LIBERALISM:
ITS CAUSE AND CURE

The Poisoning of American Christianity and the Antidote

Gregory L. Jackson

NORTHWESTERN PUBLISHING HOUSE
Milwaukee, Wisconsin

Fourth printing, 2001
Third printing, 1995
Second printing, 1992

Library of Congress Card 90-61924
Northwestern Publishing House
1250 N. 113th St., Milwaukee, WI 53226-3284
© 1991 Northwestern Publishing House
Published 1991
Printed in the United States of America
ISBN 0-8100-0356-2

DEDICATION

The orthodox Christian faith is known to us because God used faithful servants, who suffered great hardships, to hand down his word to our generation. Although many despise the word and neglect the sacraments today, our greatest privilege is to transmit the truth of God, unalloyed, to the next generation, so that the Holy Spirit might preserve their faith in Christ, the Son of God, until they are united with us at his throne. Therefore, this book is dedicated to: Allen and Ida Jackson; Paul and Sarah Webber; Titus and Julius Buelow; Ben, Andrew, Amy, and Carolyn Schmelling; Katy, Jon, Ben, and Christopher Bartsch.

CONTENTS

INTRODUCTION

This book began as an attempt to explain to the ordinary church member the corruption of the Christian faith. As Martin Chemnitz said in his *Examination of the Council of Trent,* "These are the last and mad times of a world grown old" (Part I, p 50). The typical church member does not understand how a minister could deny the virgin birth of Christ or explain away the meaning of the cross and yet remain a pastor. Nevertheless, the oldest denominations in America, commonly known as the mainline churches, are now dominated by religious leaders who have turned away from the faith they once confessed. The biblical term for turning away is apostasy (2 Thessalonians 2:3), but this sign of the end is also known as modernism or liberalism. Lutheran apostasy is treated extensively in *What's Going Wrong Among the Lutherans?*, a book which prompted many of the topics in this volume.

In order to appreciate why ministers are having prayer vigils to support abortion on demand or expressing solidarity for a pastor accused of sex abuse, one must study the history of American Christianity to discover how the wrong use of reason became a weapon of destruction against biblical faith.

The first chapter, "Decline of the Mainline Churches: the Merry Widow Waltz," shows how attacking the inerrancy of the Bible became a fixation of the mainline church leaders. The second chapter, "Merger Mania: Becoming Unitarian," discusses how the liberal interpretation of the Bible spread through the political process of denominational merger. Evolution has been used to argue for a new view of the Bible and morality, so the third chapter outlines the American Christian promotion of Darwin's theory and a possible response from Darwin's own research. Since conservative Christians often feel intimidated by logical tricks of well educated liberals, "Defending Morality" exposes the logical fallacies used to promote doubtful claims of truth. Many conservative Christians have turned to charismatic and Pentecostal groups for support, so they need to realize the close relationship between liberals and charismatics, the topic of chapter four.

"The Cure" offers the antidote to the poisoning of the Christian faith, the means of grace, as taught by the Bible, defended by the church fathers, confessed by the conservative Lutheran Reformation, and handed down to us by our pastors and teachers.

Many people have helped and encouraged me with this project, offering suggestions and improvements: Clem Haberman, Dr. Paul Boehlke, Patricia Leppien, Pastor Timothy Buelow, Pastor David Jay Webber, Rev. James Schaefer, Rev.G. Jerome Albrecht, Henry Ellenberger, my wife Chris, and my son Martin.

"So is my word that goes out from my mouth: It will not return to me empty, but will accomplish what I desire and achieve the purpose for which I sent it" (Isaiah 55:11).

Pastor Gregory L. Jackson
The Epiphany of Our Lord, 1991

1.

DECLINE OF THE MAINLINE CHURCHES: THE MERRY WIDOW WALTZ

Dean Inge, a noted theologian, said, "The church which marries the Spirit of the Age will find herself a widow in the Age to come." In a sentence, Inge described the catastrophic decline of all mainline church bodies during the last century, a merry widow waltz at an ever-increasing speed. Loss of membership, loss of influence, and loss of financial strength in the mainline churches have been so great that *Time* magazine made the subject a feature story.[1] According to the Gallup organization, mainline membership has shown a major decline since 1967. Methodist preference is down from 14% to 9%. Baptists decreased from 21% to 20%. Lutheran preference dropped from 7% to 6%. Episcopalians sank from 3% to 2%. Presbyterian preference plummeted from 6% to 3%. "No preference" jumped from 2% in 1967 to 9% in 1988. [2]

The mainline (or liberal) churches are commonly defined as those denominations which have the longest history in America: the United Church of Christ, the Presbyterian Church in the U.S.A., the United Methodist Church, the Episcopal Church, the Disciples of Christ, the Reformed Church in America, the American Baptist Conference, and the Evangelical Lutheran Church in America. Most of them share the following characteristics: use of the historical-critical method in the study of Scriptures, a history of abandoning former confessional standards through merger, membership in the National Council of Churches and the World Council of Churches, and a positive attitude toward the Social Gospel movement. The Roman Catholic Church, while not considered a mainline denomination, has taken on many of the characteristics of liberal Protestantism by adopting the same historical-critical approach to the Scriptures.

Some people wrongly assume that the hallmarks of radicalism, now flaunted by bishops of various denominations, are the result of the ferment of the 1960s. They are a century late. The 1960s simply revealed some of the long-festering weaknesses of an alien religion, an anti-Christianity which still goes by the name of liberal Christianity.

Many people were awakened to the radical nature of the mainline denominations when various members of the National Council of Churches vied with each other in ordaining active homosexuals. Other believers have been disturbed over the moral and financial support given by their own church bodies to abortion on demand. Still others have been dismayed by the uncritical attitude toward Marxism and liberation theology on the part of their world mission executives. In addition, the members find almost no emphasis on worship, evangelism, or family values.

Those who fled the mainline churches for the television evangelists found themselves equally shocked by revelations of gross financial mismanagement, prostitution, and homosexuality. They thought they had found a safe harbor from the doctrinal chaos of the mainline churches, not knowing they had simply identified with another form of liberalism, Pentecostalism.

Even the most liberal member of the most liberal denomination is likely to be shocked and horrified to learn that few mainline theology professors believe in the virgin birth of Christ. A member of Planned Parenthood doubled over in horror, holding her stomach, upon learning this, even though she scarcely went to her mainline church at all.

Although social issues, such as abortion and homosexuality, have stirred mainline members to action, the substance of the problem is not the erratic course taken by church leaders on these issues, but rather the approach taken in studying and teaching the Bible. Those people who have formed conservative caucuses on the issues have found themselves speaking another language than that of their denominational leaders. Nothing they do seems to budge the executives and seminary professors. In fact, the opposition of conservatives seems to be relished by mainline leaders, serving only to encourage even more destructive decisions. The history of biblical scholarship explains why the polarization between mainline members and ministers has taken place.

The denial of the divinity of Christ is the fruit of higher criticism, commonly known as biblical scholarship, or the historical-critical method. (In the Christian Book Distributor catalog, the traditional commentaries which assume the inerrancy of Scripture are not labeled as scholarship, but the works of the liberal publication houses, which state that the Bible is full of errors, are listed as scholarly works.) Higher criticism has some basic unwarranted assumptions which serve as the foundation for most works of biblical scholarship:

1. The Bible is a book like any other book, no more inspired by God than *Gone With the Wind*.
2. Historical statements recorded in the Bible are not reliable.

3. Accurate prophecies must have been written after the fact.
4. Jesus was not the Son of God and did not consider himself the Son of God.
5. The miraculous events of the Bible (the creation, the plagues preceding the Exodus, the virgin birth, and the resurrection of Christ) were not the work of God but coincidences or the invention of man.
6. Divine acts can be described as "myths," with the explanation that they have power in their effect upon the religious imagination, whether the events happened or not.

These rationalistic theses evolved in Europe among a few professors who stood almost alone in their peculiar views. Now most of the Protestant ministers and Catholic priests in America are trained with these anti-Christian views and subtly teach them in their churches. Mainline Bible study programs are based upon these anti-scriptural ideas.Therefore, mainline members who take these courses to learn more about the Bible end up in having their faith undermined in subtle ways.

Reimarus: Liberal Hero

Blame Reimarus, a German professor who died in 1768, leaving the German author Gotthold Lessing to publish the famous Reimarus or Wolfenbuettel *Fragments* posthumously. Reimarus, who did not believe in the divinity of Christ, contended that much of the New Testament was a pious fabrication. What he could not explain rationally, he rejected altogether.

The rationalist believes that people with psychosomatic illnesses were healed by Jesus in this way: after imagining they were sick, they started thinking they were well. Lazarus, who imagined himself dead, eventually considered himself alive! The feeding of the 5,000 was easily explained: the crowd hid their lunches until the boy shared his meager fare. Stricken by his generosity, they hauled out their own sandwiches and had baskets of leftovers. A miracle of sharing! This rationalistic explanation has been used many times in the mainline churches to support stewardship, although the miracle has nothing to do with sharing and everything to do with the power of the Son of God.

The solution to the problem of discussing the content of the Bible without believing the truth of the Scriptures was solved by David F. Strauss, a lone wolf who argued for the mythological approach to the Bible in his *Life of Jesus,* 1835. The mythological school, still very popular, simply asserts that the deeper meaning of the miraculous event does not depend on whether or not it happened. Some argued that the miracles were simply natural events which were exaggerated in the minds of the witnesses. Ernst Renan popularized this "naturalistic" perspective in his *Life of Jesus,* 1863. Fortress Press has published many of these liberal lives of Jesus in a special series. Some of them are:

Hermann S. Reimarus, *Fragments;*
Shailer Mathews, *Jesus on Social Institutions;*
Shirley Jackson Case, *Jesus, A New Biography;*
D. F. Strauss, *The Christ of Faith and the Jesus of History*; and
Friedrich Schleiermacher, *Life of Jesus.*

Albert Schweitzer, winner of the Nobel Peace Prize, summarized the German research in his *History of the Life-of-Jesus Research* (the German title translated literally), better known as *The Quest of the Historical Jesus,* 1906. Schweitzer identified with the Unitarians.

The innocent bystander looks upon these weighty tomes as paying homage to the Savior, and, in a backhanded way, they do. But the intent is clearest in the D. F. Strauss title, where the Christ of faith is distinguished from the Jesus of history. These higher critics wrote with the assumption they could find the kernel of history, the real dope on Jesus, somewhere within the myths, legends, and fables of the New Testament. Those who delve into the scholarly journals of the period can find an endless supply of articles asking whether Jesus considered himself the Messiah. Almost all of the articles and books answer, "No."

The Lutheran retreat from the inerrancy of Scriptures is discussed in great detail in Kurt Marquart's *Anatomy of an Explosion* and Craig Stanford's *The Death of the Lutheran Reformation.* The betrayal of Evangelicals on this issue is treated in Harold Lindsell's *The Battle for the Bible* and Francis Schaeffer's *The Great Evangelical Disaster*. The history of the topic is covered in *Challenges to Inerrancy*, edited by Gordon Lewis and Bruce Demarest, and *Inerrancy and the Church,* edited by John Hannah.[3]

Historical-Critical Method

In order to understand the denial of the divinity of Christ, the traditional study of Scriptures must be compared to the "modern, scholarly" historical-critical method, also known as "higher criticism." The traditional method, commonly called the historical-grammatical method, was used by the early church fathers, Luther, and the founders of the mainline Protestant denominations. The modern style of biblical study, the historical-critical method, was borrowed from a trend in the study of Greek and Latin literature. This trend, of trying to find multiple authors and influences in each work of literature, was abandoned by the classical scholars as rather useless but continues to be the norm of modern biblical study. A comparison below shows how the historical-critical method masquerades as scholarship while begging the question. (See "Popular Logical Fallacies" for examples of begging the question, commonly called circular reasoning.)

HISTORICAL-GRAMMATICAL	HISTORICAL-CRITICAL
Leaders: church fathers, Luther, the reformers.	Wellhausen, Bultmann.
Denominations: Wisconsin Evangelical Lutheran Synod, Evangelical Lutheran Synod, and various small conservative denominations.	Unitarian, Roman Catholic, U. Presbyterian, American Baptist, Southern Baptist, Disciples of Christ, Evangelical Lutheran Church in America, Reformed Church in America, Episcopalian, etc.
Sees the Bible as a whole. The Bible is inspired. The Bible is the Word of God.	Views Bible in fragments. The Bible is just a book. The Bible contains man's word about God.
The Bible contains no errors or contradictions.	The Bible is full of errors and contradictions.
The Bible is the norm of faith.	Only some parts of the Bible are normative.
Moses wrote the first five books of the Bible.	The books of Moses were written or edited by J, E, D, and P.
The Biblical accounts of divine activity are true.	All acts of God are mythical and not reliable, though some may be true.
The proper meaning of the text may be obtained from knowing the grammar of the passage and the historical setting. The Bible is clear and sufficient for our faith.	The real meaning of the passage is derived from isolating the true elements from later additions. Only an expert, a "scholar," can reach some tentative conclusions about any given text.

Most laity have an innate sense about the proper method of reading Scripture. They interject, when the divinity of Christ is denied by mainline theologians, "But isn't it clear that Jesus considered himself the Messiah? Doesn't the Bible clearly teach that Jesus was born of a virgin *young maiden* and that he rose from the dead?"

One can only reply, "You are talking another language. You believe the Bible is the Word of God, his clear and infallible revelation, sufficient and authoritative. They consider the Bible another book, not very well written, full of errors and contradictions."

Yale and the Progress of Higher Criticism

Yale University was founded in 1701, "conservative before she was born," in the words of Roland Bainton.[4] When Yale was founded, New Englanders were naming their children Ichabod, because the glory of Israel was departed (Ichabod means the glory has departed, 1 Samuel 4:21). The Calvinism of the founding fathers was being watered down. Harvard was already degenerate.

Jonathan Edwards was one of the most famous graduates of Yale, a school founded to provide both civil and religious leadership for New England. Edwards' grandson, Timothy Dwight the Elder, became president of Yale in 1795 and lectured students in the basics of Christianity, leading to a genuine religious awakening after eight years of effort. Dwight's *Theology Explained*, 5 volumes, 1818, became a classic of the era. His hymn, "I Love Thy Kingdom, Lord," is in *The Lutheran Hymnal*. Timothy Dwight the Younger, grandson of the Elder, studied higher criticism in Europe but still taught the old methods at Yale when Benjamin Bacon was a student.

Benjamin Bacon

How was biblical instruction carried out at Yale when Benjamin Bacon studied there at the turn of the century? Bacon himself described it:

1) That the apostle John wrote the fourth Gospel was considered established for all time;
2) Objections to the Mosaic authorship of the Pentateuch were dismissed as the work of hostile critics;
3) The historical-grammatical method, used by Luther, was dominant, and liberalism was rebuked.[5]

Bacon saw the Yale of his youth as battling rearguard actions. Yale Divinity, after the Civil War, was like the seminaries of conservative denominations today. However, when Dwight died in 1916, the age of conservative biblical scholarship in the mainline churches was drawing to an end. The traditional faith represented by Jonathan Edwards, Timothy Dwight the Elder, and Timothy Dwight the Younger ceased to matter.

Bacon started teaching at Yale in 1881 after serving as a Congregationalist minister for 13 years. Bacon combined the three German schools of higher criticism in his treatment of the feeding of the 5,000. Following Paulus, using a rationalistic interpretation, Bacon explained the abundance of food as the sharing of hidden food. Copying D. F. Strauss' mythological method, Bacon saw the "legendary" elements as derived from the Old Testament accounts of Elisha feeding 100 men (2 Kings 4:42-44). Emulating F. C. Bauer's effort to find the real story behind the story, Bacon discerned in the narrative a group of early Christian controversies being settled.[6]

If Bacon was so free with the text, what did he actually believe? There are some hints in *Yale and the Ministry*. The Congregationalist magazine reported humorously in 1911 that Bacon was put through a mock trial, the charge being—orthodoxy![7]

Bainton reported that Bacon and another professor

made Dean Charles Brown, a Social Gospel advocate, doubtful about the Virgin Birth. When questioned about his faith, Brown "handled the question with superb finesse. He would say, 'What do I believe about the virgin birth? Exactly what the Apostle Paul believed. And what did he believe? He never mentioned it.' "8

The New Scholarship at Yale

Bacon was not entirely to blame for the shift at Yale. Such dramatic changes required institutional approval by now-forgotten board members. A key change came about when Yale Divinity was at its lowest ebb, in 1905, when Edward L.Curtis was appointed acting dean. Curtis had previously taught at the Presbyterian seminary, McCormick in Chicago, where he alienated conservatives. (McCormick is thoroughly liberal today.) Curtis battled for the new methods and theories. In his work on Chronicles in the *International Critical Commentary,* he judged the books worthless as history but valuable for their idealized version of the past. Bainton wrote: "After coming to Yale, Curtis put to flight armies of aliens in the battle for higher criticism."9

In 1886, George Barker Stevens began teaching New Testament at Yale. Stevens, now largely forgotten, denied the veracity of the Gospel of John and rejected the atonement of Christ. Yale Divinity gradually became an interdenominational school, abandoned its prescribed creed for professors, and became much more open to the winds of change. When Douglas C. Macintosh was hired in 1907, the only question asked which was remotely related to theology involved his position on close communion.10

The Social Gospel movement, which borrowed its Brotherhood of Man and Fatherhood of God theology from the European liberals, arrived at Yale at the same approximate time as the new style of biblical criticism. In 1887, Washington Gladden, a minister from Columbus, Ohio, gave the Lyman Beecher lectures at Yale. In 1917, Walter Rauschenbusch gave the lectures which continue to be published as *A Theology for the Social Gospel*. Those three decades, 1887-1917, established the Social Gospel as the definitive form of American Protestantism. Although the terminology and agenda have changed over the years, the Pelagianism (man saves himself) of the Social Gospel movement has persevered, corrupting every denomination enchanted with so-called modern biblical scholarship.

Although it was fashionable to pooh-pooh Rauschenbusch soon after he lectured at Yale, he distilled the theology and aims of liberalism with superb prose and moving stories. To this day people in graduate school are judged by their admiration for Rauschenbusch. One critical remark can render the graduate suspect in the eyes of the professor. Rauschenbusch thought he was accomplishing a great good for mankind and the church, but his horrible distortion of the Christian faith damaged the core of Christian teaching. He considered himself an evangelist and felt he was rescuing Christianity from oblivion.

A brief summary of Rauschenbusch's theology can help the innocent observer of the church scene see how corrupted theology was already in 1917. Rauschenbusch was not too sure about the origin of evil, relying as he did on the historical-critical assumption of J,E,P,D as authors of the Pentateuch. His thoughts on personal salvation have nothing to do with salvation by grace, but focus instead on whether the "converted" person is good enough to be accepted into the church, whether he has the right notions, affinities, ideals.

The social gospel furnishes new tests for religious experience. We are not disposed to accept the converted souls whom the individualistic evangelism supplies, without looking them over.[11]

In a previous work, Rauschenbusch had harsh words for Dr. Friedrich Pfotenhauer (1859-1939), the last truly conservative president of the Missouri Synod, who served from 1911 to 1935.

In *Theology,* Rauschenbusch praised Christian Science, perhaps aware that the dean of Yale Divinity, Charles Brown, was a certified healer with a diploma from Mrs. Eddy.[12] Though he praised the fading light of Christian Science, Rauschenbusch rejected the accuracy of the Scriptures. He wrote that instances of Jesus' use of "church" were in passages of doubtful authenticity.[13] He also sharply distinguished between the intentions of Jesus (as he saw them) and the claims of the church—the Jesus of history as distinguished from the Christ of faith.

Rauschenbusch used the kingdom of God as his central concept, not in the sense of the invisible church, the body of believers, but in the sense of those areas where God's justice is established by man. This is the central motive power of mainline Christianity today, that man must use the power of the church to redeem society, through legislation and boycotts, quotas and petitions, Russian assault rifles, and condoms. Rauschenbusch utterly rejected the biblical concept of inspiration, claiming bitterly that it "quenched the Spirit." [14] Needless to say, Rauschenbusch rejoiced in the fruits of the historical-critical method.

The last few pages of *Theology* contain the most destructive bit of propaganda published in this century. There Rauschenbusch distinguished between the prophet (himself, Jesus, and other good guys) and the priest (the Pharisees, conservatives, and other bad guys). "The priest is a religious professional." He lusts for power, rewrites history (the Bible), and opposes free expression. He is a middleman, a selfish exploiter of religion.[15] In contrast, Rauschenbusch concluded from his study of history:

> The prophet becomes a prophet by some personal experience of God, which henceforth is the dominant reality of his life. It creates inward convictions which become his message to men. Usually after great inward conflicts and the bursting of priest-made barriers he discovered the way of access to God, and has found him wonderful,—just, merciful, free.[16]

By identifying Jesus with this peculiar notion of the prophet, and by connecting suffering with the prophetical to end all social injustice, Rauschenbusch ignited fires which have since burned fiercely in the mainline denominations.

Every mainline pastor who assaulted a congregation with salvation-by-works sermons earned, thanks to Rauschenbusch, the right to call himself a prophet. All opposition, the mainline seminarian was told, was due to those selfish priests and their mindless slaves. While many self-appointed prophets found other callings in time, enough survived the doctrinal wars of the last 50 years to become denominational presidents, seminary professors, board chairmen, agency directors, college presidents, and pastors of large congregations. Others found that paying lip service to social activism and remaining silent about doctrinal problems earned rewards and prevented trouble.

The original Social Gospel agenda was basically the New Deal of President Franklin Roosevelt: labor laws to protect union members, a minimum wage, pure food and drug legislation, child labor laws, social insurance for the elderly and disabled, justice for farmers, and repudiation of war. The first *Superman* comic book, issued in 1938, showed the influence of the Social Gospel agenda. Superman dealt with unfair labor practices, cheating in football, and obscene profits enjoyed by an armaments manufacturer who fomented war to increase business. The Social Gospel agenda was established first by the Methodist Church, in its Social Creed, later adopted by the Federal Council of Churches in the early 1900s.

The Federal Council of Churches was organized to serve as the institutional arm of the Social Gospel movement, uniting the liberal Protestant churches in an integrated effort to use their power to bring in the kingdom of God. After too many Reds were found under the bed, the FCC was reorganized as the National Council of Churches in 1948. The National Council of Churches helped spawn the World Council of Churches, whose work was pioneered by earlier ecumenical movements.

The National and World Councils of Churches are officially separate but cross-pollinate frequently and share the same headquarters in New York City. Statewide councils of churches and local ecumenical forums blanket the nation with a network of activist ministers and laity who join efforts to lobby for peace and justice legislation and to boycott certain businesses.

Even more fertilization is provided by the Geneva, Switzerland, headquarters of the World Alliance of Reformed Churches and the Lutheran World Federation. The World Council of Churches is also located in Geneva and works with LWF and WARC. The groups share the same doctrinal indifference, the same identification of social activism with real Christianity, and the same enthusiasm for Marxist analysis of societal problems.

For theology, the Depression was judgment day, the fulfillment of what the Social Gospel had predicted. The 1930s brought about changes in seminaries and denominations, radical departures already established at Yale, Harvard, and Union. Princeton abandoned its Calvinistic conservatism in the 1930s. At the same time, the Lutheran Church Missouri Synod was attacked from within for being out of date and too dogmatic. The Augustana Synod changed its faculty in 1931, moving toward the day when they could merge with the doctrinally vague United Lutheran Church in America.

In each case, the battles won at Yale, Harvard, and Union were replayed in the tiny, obscure seminaries of America, where the bright young professors basked in the glory of their earned doctorates. They were not the bearded old conservative fogies of their denomination's dark past.They were modern scholars in their own right, with publications (usually heavily subsidized by the denomination's printing house) independent of criticism from "reactionary Fundamentalists."

Yes, the liberals sighed, the battles were tough, but once the younger clergy were trained in the new methods, the denomination would take off into new flights of creative social activism. The progressives worked very hard, practiced the strictest form of excommunication and fellowship, promoted one another and never ceased to make converts out of believers.

The process of undermining the faith of the clergy has been gradual, working best where unnoticed. The more conservative denominations of the Midwest were not affected at first. They were established by the wave of immigrants in the middle of the last century, when Iowa was still the frontier. Unlike their mainline counterparts, which had already Americanized, the new denominations continued to work in their mother tongues.

The new Americans started their own colleges and seminaries. They were isolated from the trends in the mainline seminaries. An Ivy League education was not valued at first. Instead, doctrinal fidelity and denominational respect earned pastors a place in teaching.

Later, a degree from Yale, Harvard, or Princeton seemed to lend prestige to a tiny seminary or college.

As time passed, a Ph. D. was required of all professors, but doctrinal fidelity was considered a throwback to the dark ages, when old Prof. Johnson or Zweig spoke with a funny accent and displayed his obsolete perspective by denouncing evolution and doctrinal aberrations.

The historical-critical drama was replayed in each denomination and each seminary. Some became angry and quit, thereby making the next step toward infidelity easier. If a walkout was organized so that large numbers left at once, the liberals rejoiced at losing so much ballast so effortlessly. The ecumenical nature of graduate study served to draw denominations together, especially those with similar ethnic or confessional ties. Leaders also had a common bond in their complaints about reactionaries who resisted their new ideas. While the conservatives of various denominations avoided one another because of their practice of fellowship principles, the liberals worked with each other at many different levels, finding common ground in their progressive views.

Educational Victories

The capture of the newer colleges and seminaries by the historical-critical method had a slow but profound effect on each denomination. College and seminary professors have a lasting influence on their students, especially upon ministers, who remain students all their lives. One Yale Divinity professor observed, "I can tell what year a minister graduated from seminary by looking at his library." The bulk of a minister's library will be purchased during college and seminary, when he has the most time to study. His reference books, especially the biblical commentaries, will become familiar to him during those formative years. If he enters college believing in the inerrancy of the Bible and the divinity of Christ, a different perspective will either convert him or drive him away. Either reaction is a victory for the historical-critical method, since both alternatives purify the denomination of rejected views.

A minister's office will be filled with books which teach the infallible truths of the word of God, as Luther did, or attack those truths. The two different approaches can best be illustrated by the experience of one young man entering seminary. One pastor took him aside and said, "Remember this, no matter what happens, always stay with the Word of God and study it closely. Never depart from it." A mainline pastor took the same student into his study for "a lesson you can use throughout your whole ministry." What followed was a demonstration on how to open a new book without hurting the binding. Or, as one pastor noted, confessional ministers say, "God's blessings" to each other, while mainline pastors say, "Good luck."

College and seminary students want to be regarded as good students. Few, if any, want to stand out as difficult students. If they begin with a simple Sunday school attitude toward Jesus, then a complex, adult, scholarly perspective seems far better. If their denomination is just moving toward the historical-critical method, only a light touch is used. The divinity of Christ is left alone, but the historicity of Adam and Eve is left open. The professor may simply say, "Is it possible that Adam and Eve are symbolic of mankind?"

When a college and seminary have been thoroughly modernized, the student has only the tomes of the historical-critical method to read. The seminary bookstore does not sell the old books based upon the inerrancy of Scripture, if they are still in print. The professors mention them only to scoff or to offer faint praise. "Lenski really knew his Greek, but he is outdated."

The educational situation seems ideally suited for the promotion of false doctrine. If the seminary is deeply committed to teaching the denomination's confession of faith, it must also show its students how to identify and refute false doctrine. The students must therefore read the classics of the historical-critical school and understand their approach.

If the seminary, however, is committed to the historical-critical method, the students are told to avoid the old books, if they are told anything at all. No one is told, "My predecessor in New Testament believed in the divinity of Christ, but I don't." Students are brought along slowly, until the denomination is so packed with progressives that a debate on doctrine will turn into accusations of disturbing the tranquility of the church, hurting the finances of the school, or trying to gain a reputation at the expense of others.

Pietistic Bridge

Midwestern Lutherans have seen their denominations move from conservatism to radicalism within one generation. Many of them went to colleges which forbade dancing, cardplaying, and movies. They remember straightlaced professors who never expressed a doubt about the Bible, whether in a class on Christianity or in the biology lab. Now the same institutions seem to glow with pride in adopting the worst excesses of the mainline denominations. In fact, through merger, the ethnic colleges of Lutheran pietism have become mainline members.

The pietistic movement had a great impact on all Lutheran groups, but especially on the Midwestern churches, made up of Germans, Swedes, Norwegians, Finns, and Danes. Pietism began with the work of Philip Jacob Spener, whose *Pia Desideria* in 1635 set forth a six-point program for improving the piety of Christians. It included 1) more diligent Bible study, 2) application of doctrine of the priesthood of all believers, 3) an emphasis on deed rather than doctrine, 4) an emphasis on prayer for the erring and unbelieving rather than theological debates, 5) reform of seminary studies with a greater role for personal piety, 6) a devotional arrangement of sermons. Unlike Luther, Spener did not hold that heaven and earth depended on every point of doctrine. Influenced by Reformed theologians, Spener rejected the Real Presence of Christ in the Lord's Supper. Likewise, the Pietists denied baptismal regeneration, along with the Reformed.[17]

Spener and his successor at Halle University in Germany, Francke, pioneered the lay-led Bible study and prayer groups that characterize Pietism. Halle became the center of Pietism, training thousands of clergy, including Henry Melchior Muhlenberg, through whom Lutheran pietism was established in the General Synod in America.

Adolf Hoenecke pointed out the fundamental flaw of Pietism:

> *Wohl scheint auf den ersten Blick die ganze Differenz recht unbedeutend; aber in Wahrheit gibt sich hier die gefaehrliche Richtung der Pietisten zu erkennen, das Leben ueber die Lehre, die Heiligung ueber die Rechtfertigung und die Froemmigkeit nicht als Folge, sondern als Bedingung der Erleuchtung zu setzen, also eine Art Synergismus und Pelagianismus einzufuehren.* (At first glance, the total difference seems absolutely insignificant, but in truth the dangerous direction of Pietism is made apparent: life over doctrine, sanctification over justification, and piety not as a consequence but declared as a condition of enlightenment, introducing a kind of synergism and Pelagianism.) [18]

When the Scandinavian and German Lutherans settled the Midwest, they were influenced largely by the Pietism of their countries. While the emphasis on rejecting the worldliness of their homelands seemed laudable, the lax attitude toward correct doctrine and the Lutheran confessions worked like leaven through each group.

At the heart of the Pietistic dilemma was the conflict between confessional Lutheranism and the Reformed influence which insisted upon the proper evidence of the Christian life. One could not put a carefully prescribed life first and also make correct doctrine the first priority. Because Pietism influenced all Protestant groups, the Lutheran Pietists often saw great affinities with others who supported the Temperance Movement and other social causes. Working together promoted doctrinal tolerance and diversity.

Since Lutheran Pietism emphasized Bible study over correct interpretation of the Bible, advocates of the historical-critical method had an easy time in using such piety against the historic stance of inerrancy. Bible study groups and Sunday school teachers were slowly introduced to the claims of the historical-critical method. When presented by a pastor who would never drink a beer or play a hand of Old Maid, the new claims seemed sanctified by a holy life. Such a pastor might present Jonah as a parable, but never suggest that Jesus died for nothing.

Because Pietism resonated with Reformed doctrine, Lutherans who were swept up in the movement placed a greater degree of emphasis on feeling saved and doing sanctified works than on the objective means of grace. The unfortunate and artificial split between head and heart knowledge, deed and creed, prepared the Pietists for the clandestine assaults of modernism. A later Swedish Pietist, Peter Waldenstroem, 1838-1917, began a new denomination in America by attacking the Atonement. Heick, a historian of doctrine, noted:

> His theology bears a close resemblance to the teaching of Albrecht Ritschl. He is a striking example of the fact that a pietistic way of life

and theological liberalism may go a long way together.[19]

One can see that even with the Social Gospel movement, the earnest desire to make a difference in society was a hallmark of the influence of Pietism. By emphasizing the outward signs of the faith while disregarding the pure doctrine of the Bible, Christians lost the gospel by adding the law.

The Fruit

What has been the result of this vast effort? How can we measure the fruits of liberalism? The seminaries of mainline Protestantism and Roman Catholicism teach future ministers to doubt the truth of the Bible and the certainty of their salvation. The offerings of faithful Christians are diverted from genuine gospel ministry to support political lobbying, abortion on demand, homosexuality, and worldwide terrorism. Mainline church leaders, united by efforts of the National Council of Churches, clamor to oppose American foreign policy actions while supporting the intentions of the Soviets. Court cases to support the free exercise of religion, as guaranteed in the Bill of Rights, are countered by briefs from mainline churches working in concert with the American Civil Liberties Union and Norman Lear's People for the American Way. Through the Religious Coalition for Abortion Rights, denominational executives gather to sign statements declaring that abortion is a religious right. Mainline campus ministries use their positions to promote radical left-wing activities at colleges across the nation. Homosexual ministers receive unctious blessings from clergy while launching vicious assaults on the Bible. Legend has it that when Julian the Apostate died in 363, after failing to make the Roman Empire pagan again, his final words were, "Galilean, you have conquered." Now many are tempted to murmur instead, "Reimarus, you have conquered."

NOTES

1. Richard Ostling, "Those Mainline Blues, " May 22, 1989, pp. 94-96. See also *Newsweek* cover story, Dec. 17, 1990.
2. *The Northwestern Lutheran*, May 1, 1988, p. 174.
3. *Anatomy of an Explosion, A Theological Analysis of the Missouri Synod Conflict*, Grand Rapids: Baker Book House, 1977. Craig S. Stanford, *The Death of the Lutheran Reformation, A Practical Look at Modern Theology and its Effects in the Church and in the Lives of its People,* Ft. Wayne: Stanford Publishing, 1988; *The Battle for the Bible,* Grand Rapids: Zondervan, 1976; *The Great Evangelical Disaster,*Westchester, Illinois: Crossway Books, 1984; *Challenges to Inerrancy, A Theological Response,* Chicago: Moody Press, 1984; *Inerrancy and the Church*, Chicago: Moody Press, 1984.
4. *Yale and the Ministry,* New York: Harper, 1957, pp. 1f.
5. Bainton, ibid., p. 174.
6. Ibid., pp. 214f.
7. Ibid., p. 204.
8. Ibid., p. 207. Bainton's merriment over the confessional agility of Dean Brown is obvious. Bainton's *Yesterday, Today, and What Next?*, is an attack on the Christian faith, published by the Augsburg Publishing House, 1978.

   A fine book for appreciating mythological interpretation is *Kerygma and Myth,* by Rudolph Bultmann and Five Critics, New York: Harper and Row, 1961. Because Herman Sasse, a conservative Lutheran, seemed critical of the mythological approach, "essays which take Sasse's line" were omitted from the *Kerygma and Myth* volume (p. ix).
9. Ibid., p. 179.
10. Ibid., p. 203.
11. *A Theology for the Social Gospel*, New York: Abingdon Press, 1945, p. 96. Rauschenbusch taught at Rochester Divinity School, which is now merged into several other divinity schools. Rauschenbusch's father was Lutheran and could have become a founder of the Wisconsin Synod. The father's conversion to the Baptist perspective prevented that outcome. J. P. Koehler, *History of the Wisconsin Synod,* published by the Protéstant Conference, Sauk Rapids: Sentinel Publishing, 1981, pp. 36, 39.
12. Theology, p. 121. Bainton, op. cit., p. 205.
13. Theology, p. 131.
14. Ibid., p. 192.
15. Ibid., p. 275.

16. Ibid.
17. Otto Heick, *History of Christian Thought,* 2 vols.
18. *Evangelische-Lutherische Dogmatik,* 4 vols., ed., Walter and Otto Hoenecke,Milwaukee: Northwestern Publishing House, 1912, III, p. 253. See also Ernst Wendland, "Present-Day Pietism," *Wisconsin Lutheran Quarterly,* vol. 49 (1952), pp. 19-35.
19. Heick, op. cit., II, p. 218.

2.

MERGER MANIA: BECOMING UNITARIAN

Houdini, the famous magician, used to astound people by having himself locked in a safe and then escaping. From working at a factory that made safes, Houdini knew what the audience did not, that safes were weaker on the inside than on the outside. For the same reason, Christianity has withstood centuries of attack from the outside, growing stronger in the process. In the last century, however, the Christian faith has been attacked from within, by those who know where the weak places are. The attacks have come from self-described liberals who lead denominations and inter-denominational agencies, teach in church-owned colleges and seminaries, and serve as pastors in congregations. Liberal Christianity is not Christianity at all, but an anti-Christian cult, an alien philosophy at war with the Scriptures, operating through deceit, manipulating the hearts and minds of sincere believers who mistakenly finance the destructive programs of apostasy.

Apostasy describes our era better than liberalism does, for apostasy literally means a falling away from the truth a believer once confessed. Someone who never trusted in Christ could not be called an apostate. However, a person who formerly believed in Jesus as the Son of God and Savior but now rejects the divinity of Christ, spending his energy in undermining the faith of others — that person is an apostate. While the laity of the church may stop attending services while still believing, the clergy become even more involved in the Church after losing their faith. Luther wrote:

> When a devil gets a man into his clutches who has been in our midst and also has the Bible, such an apostate is worse and more harmful than all the heathen, who know not Scripture.[1]

Apostasy is a sign of the end, predicted in 2 Thessalonians 2:1ff and 2 Timothy 3:1ff. Paul warned Timothy:

> Now the Spirit expressly says that in later times some *will depart from the faith* by giving heed to deceitful spirits and doctrines of demons, through the pretensions of liars whose consciences are seared, who forbid marriage, and enjoin abstinence from foods which God created to be received with thanksgiving by those who believe and know the truth. (1 Timothy 4:1-3 RSV)

He also wrote:

> For the time is coming when people will not endure sound teaching, but having itching ears they will accumulate for themselves teachers to suit their own likings, and will turn away from listening to the truth and wander into myths. As for you, always be steady, endure suffering, do the work of an evangelist, fulfill your ministry. (2 Timothy 4:3-5; RSV)

The most recent religious scandals have alerted people to the fact that a turning away from the truth of the Word of God has indeed taken place, and that many scoffers of all varieties have murdered the souls of countless believers by taking away their trust in Christ as Savior.

Those who study cults find a common characteristic among them, that the most basic Christian doctrines are denied: hell, the divinity of Christ, the virgin birth, the miracles, the bodily resurrection of Christ, and the Trinity. Yet cults want to be called Christian and call themselves the only true manifestation of Christianity, even while denying the doctrines of the Bible. The Masonic Lodge is an 18th-century, anti-Christian cult. Although the Masons make use of some words from the Bible, and even claim to be Christian, no one can pray in the name of Christ in a Masonic Lodge, lest he be subject to discipline. Ordinary Masons (Shriners, Knights Templar, Rainbow Girls, DeMolay) are taught that they do not belong to a religion, but the Masonic experts present the lodge system as a religion and confess it as a religion. In brief, Masons are taught that they will enter the Celestial Lodge by being good Masons.

The Mormons or Latter-day Saints, considered a renegade branch of Masonry by the Masons themselves for copying the rituals of the Lodge, are perhaps the fastest growing 20th-century cult. Mormons teach that people become gods by being good Mormons. The Mormon temple rituals are much like Masonic rites, because their first leader, Joseph Smith, was a Masonic leader. [2]

In the same way, liberalism is a cult which borrows the terminology of the Christian faith in order to extend its influence and subvert the church. How badly has the Christian faith been distorted in the last century? Consider these examples:

1. A Lutheran visited his friend at a seminary in a major city, hoping to talk about Christ. The seminarian said, "[expletive deleted], I don't know who Christ is!" The seminarian was later ordained. The Lutheran layman joined a Pentecostal group and became quite involved in world missionary activities.

2. A Presbyterian doubted the divinity of Christ and received approval for ordination. The same year, another candidate doubted the ordination of women and was turned down. Later, a Presbyterian minister was told to leave the ministry because he had expressed doubts about the ordination of women. He promised to be silent about the topic, but the church official said, "I can't risk it." The minister joined another denomination.

3. A Roman Catholic woman glowed about her brother-in-law's work as a theologian at a Roman Catholic theology school. "He wrote that there's nothing wrong with couples living together, since so many people are doing it now. And 10 per cent are homosexual. So it must be part of God's plan. The cardinal asked my brother-in-law into his office. We thought he was in trouble. The cardinal said, 'The trouble with you is that you are too honest.' The cardinal gave him a big hug before he left and said, 'Stay healthy.' "

4. A future Disciples of Christ minister said, "At our school, one third of the divinity students are Unitarian." During the conversation she made an obscene remark about the virgin birth, denied the resurrection of Christ, and dismissed both doctrines as "unimportant."

5. The hymnal committee for the United Methodist Church almost included "Strong Mother God" as an addition to its forthcoming hymnal. Feminists vowed to appeal the negative vote at the 1988 convention. An avalanche of phone calls prevented the

hymnal committee from deleting "Onward Christian Soldiers" for being too warlike.

6. The president of the Southern Baptist Church tried to ask the seminary professors at Louisville, their largest school, what they believed. They refused, claiming academic freedom. Yet the *Wall Street Journal*, considered a somewhat conservative publication, covered the Southern Baptist conflict as if the advocates of inerrancy were conducting the Salem witch trials all over again.[3]

7. A minister of a "conservative" group said he would not transfer members to churches of the same denomination in town, because of their vast doctrinal differences.

8. A professor in the liturgy program at the University of Notre Dame, Niels Rasmussen, O. P., was discovered dead in his home with a bullet in his heart. Police found equipment nearby used in sado-masochistic homosexual rituals (whips, handcuffs, leather articles). A note left by the deceased asked that no Christian burial rites be performed. William Storey, recently retired from the Notre Dame liturgy department, urged a police investigation of the case. Storey is a confessed atheist and homosexual. Notre Dame is the Vatican-approved center for teaching the theology of worship. [4]

Some people will react to such stories by saying, "These are only isolated instances, the worst possible examples anyone could dredge up." That notion would be comforting, if reality did not disturb our hope-filled illusions. A mainline seminary student brought his textbook, required for his biblical studies class, to an adult Bible study class. The book, *Understanding the New Testament,* by liberal Howard Clark Kee, claims that John's Gospel "insists that he was born in Nazareth rather than in Bethlehem (John 7:41-42) and that Joseph was his father (John 1:45)." [5]

Those who believe that television Christianity provides an alternative to liberal apostasy will find that the stars of media religion are deeply involved in the rankest false doctrine, from occultic imaging (Robert Schuller, Pat Robertson, Paul Y. Cho) to Mormon-like deification of the self (Jimmie Swaggart, Paul Crouch) and the prosperity gospel of Robert Tilton, Oral Roberts and many others.[6]

The irony of liberal Christianity is that a tiny group, the Unitarian-Universalist Association, has seen its unChristianity overwhelm the mainline church bodies. The U-U's, as they call themselves, do not need to start a lot of mission congregations or join the Church Growth Movement. The liberal church bodies have enthusiastically embraced the Unitarian-Universalist heresy.[7]

Some well-known Unitarians of the past include Susan B. Anthony, Ralph Waldo Emerson, Adlai Stevenson, Frank Lloyd Wright, Alexander Graham Bell, Albert Schweitzer, and Linus Pauling. Unitarian U. S. presidents include: John Adams, Thomas Jefferson, John Quincy Adams, Millard Fillmore, and William Howard Taft. Their total membership today is only 179,000 with slightly over 1,000 churches.[8]

A Little Unitarian History

In 1785, James Freeman, a liberal Harvard graduate, decided to improve the Book of Common Prayer, removing trinitarian references. The church was King's Chapel in Boston, the first Episcopalian congregation in America, also the first Unitarian meeting place. Apostasy, the turning away from the Christian faith, took only a liberal religious leader and an easygoing congregation. Of course, the Unitarian spirit was in the wind, blowing over from England and Poland. Even in the time of Luther, the Socinians (mentioned in the Augsburg Confession) were actively denying Christian doctrine.

Benjamin Franklin believed in a creator, in the immortality of the soul, and eternal life—enough to get him removed from the most prestigious theological faculties today for being a Fundamentalist. But Franklin was not a Christian believer and did not attend church on Sunday. His rational and moral approach to life blossomed in New England.

When two moderate Calvinists at Harvard died, in 1803 and 1804, Jedidiah Morse demanded publicly that orthodox men replace them. Instead, after a long battle, liberal professors replaced them. The acrimony which followed helped uncover latent Unitarianism, which is based on a rationalistic approach to the Bible, rejecting the Trinity, the divinity of Christ, his pre-existence, the virgin birth, his miracles, his atoning death, and his resurrection.

Morse, a Yale graduate, could see what was blowing into New England through Harvard and set about creating Andover Divinity School as an orthodox antidote to Harvard. He continued his remorseless attack on liberalism by quoting an English Unitarian's glowing account of apostasy in America. The "quiet and dignified" William E. Channing lamented this effort in an open letter where he used the term Unitarian. Like all liberals, Channing argued that his version of Christianity was the true faith.[9]

By 1819, Unitarianism was in full flower. The Unitarian congregations devolved from the Congregationalist parishes influenced by their Harvard-trained pastors. Yale graduates like Moses Stuart, a Hebrew scholar, countered the Harvard menace, and Unitarianism was confined largely to the "Fatherhood of God, the Brotherhood of Man and the neighborhood of Boston," as people have joked. Some Congregationalist parishes split over doctrinal issues. Others slowly became Unitarian by the gradual process of doctrinal laxity and corruption. The political process added congregations to the Unitarian association as well.

Park Street Church in Boston was organized as a counter to Unitarianism, to preserve the Christian faith and retain a conservative Protestant approach. The recently deceased Rev. Harold Ockenga served as pastor of Park Street, helped establish *Christianity Today*, Fuller Seminary, and the Billy Graham Crusades. Ockenga was a pioneer in promoting ecumenical Evangelicalism, emphasizing only the positive elements which united various confessions. This led eventually to the amalgamation of Evangelicalism, Pentecostalism, and liberalism one finds today in *Christianity Today*, the Billy Graham Crusade, and Fuller Seminary.

Stuart charged in 1819 that Unitarianism was simply a half-way house on the way to infidelity. The Unitarians, like their descendants in various denominational seminaries, were anxious to prove they believed in something.[10] In 1853 they issued a florid statement affirming that God existed and that Jesus taught the truth, if we distinguish his genuine sayings from the rest of the New Testament.

Ralph Waldo Emerson unsettled Unitarian nerves when he addressed the Harvard Divinity graduating class in 1838, declaring a pantheism which found the biblical concept of miracle a "Monster." Unitarians were still clinging to some notion of the divine, so the battle raged for decades. This was a foretaste of mainline church struggles, where similar appeals to the "cutting edge" of theology led to disintegration of doctrinal standards, in the midst of such misleading claims as this: "The Gospel means that God remains faithful even when we are not." The reference to 2 Timothy 2:13 has been used by mainline ministers to support their infidelity, rather than the faithfulness of God. Whenever a liberal denomination slips another notch into apostasy, the older liberal leaders, who greased the skids by first proposing and defending looser doctrinal standards, lament loudly the growth of destructive trends. Retired bishops can be most critical of the consequences of their action or inaction.

The first stage of Unitarianism was the denial of the divinity of Christ. The second stage of decline was signaled by Emerson's Harvard speech, confessing a pantheism which is only slightly removed from atheism. A pantheist believes that everything in the universe is god, rejecting the merciful, loving God of the Scriptures. The Unitarians were pioneers in the historical-critical method, an influence which spread to the mainline churches, as detailed in "Merry Widow Waltz."

Unitarians have the highest percentage of women clergy, 22%. More than half of the Unitarian divinity students are women. "The church is also outspoken in its defense of gays and lesbians, openly embracing them as clergy." Unitarian-Universalist minister Rev. Betty Doty said, "As a group, we do not accept Jesus Christ as our Lord and Savior."

Modern biblical scholarship in the Unitarian confession produced the Secular Humanist movement, which is outright atheism. Carl Sagan won the Humanist of the Year Award for his "Cosmos" television series, which bristled with anti-Christian remarks. One founder of Secular Humanism, which has been recognized as a religion by the U. S. Supreme Court, was Curtis Reese, who had been ordained as a Southern Baptist minister. A laudatory biographical sketch states: "Impressed by the higher criticism of the Bible, which undermined his biblical faith, he evolved intellectually toward Unitarianism and eventually declared his change of faith in 1913. . . ."[11]

Charles Potter, another Baptist minister, was smoked out by colleagues, kicked out of his denomination, and turned Unitarian. John Dietrich, who was raised in a conservative Reformed group, served as a Reformed pastor until removed from the ministry of his denomination for heresy in 1911. He also became a Unitarian minister.

Reese declared that "the outstanding characteristic of modern liberals, and indeed of all modern thinking, is the evaluation of personality as the thing of supreme worth."[12]

A Unitarian opponent of this unblemished atheism was William Sullivan, a former Roman Catholic priest who was booted out of the church for his fondness for modernism. In 1921 he led an unsuccessful "conservative" battle to get all Unitarians to declare that they believed in God. Some of the most effective Unitarian leaders have been former pastors from Christian denominations. Times have changed. Now these men would no longer have to leave their denominations to give Unitarian sermons.

The first Humanist Manifesto was drafted by Roy Wood Sellars in 1932-33 and signed by three of the ex-ministers mentioned above: Reese, Potter, and Dietrich. Augustine was correct about the decline of doctrine, even among the Unitarians. First, false doctrine is tolerated. Then, false doctrine is given an equal voice. Finally, false doctrine dominates. Today the typical Unitarian minister is likely to be an atheist who views Channing and Emerson as crusty old conservatives.

The first Humanist Manifesto declared:

> Religious humanists regard the universe as self-existing and not created. Humanism asserts that the nature of the universe depicted by modern science makes unacceptable any supernatural or cosmic guarantees of human values. Religious humanism considers the complete realization of human personality to be the end of man's life and seeks its development and fulfillment in the here and now. In the place of the old attitudes involved in worship and prayer the humanist finds his religious emotions expressed in a heightened sense of personal life and in a co-operative effort to promote social well-being. Man

is at last becoming aware that he alone is respon-
sible for the realization of the world of his
dreams, that he has within himself the power for
its achievement.[13]

Some of the original signers of the Humanist
Manifesto include Lester Mondale, the half-brother of
Walter Mondale, the former vice-president of the
United States, and John Dewey (1859-1952), the fore-
most influence in American education today.

The second Humanist Manifesto, 1973, elaborated
the implied agenda of the earlier version. The updated
version stated:

> . . . traditional dogmatic or authoritarian reli-
> gions that place revelation, God, ritual, or creed
> above human need or experience do a disservice
> to the human species . . . we can discover no
> divine purpose or providence for the human
> species. While there is much that we do not
> know, humans are responsible for what we are
> or will become. No deity will save us; we must
> save ourselves.
> We affirm that moral values derive their source
> from human experience. Ethics is autonomous
> and situational, needing no theological or ideo-
> logical sanction. In the area of sexuality, we
> believe that intolerant attitudes, often culti-
> vated by orthodox religions and puritanical cul-
> tures, unduly repress sexual conduct. The
> right to birth control, abortion and divorce
> should be recognized.[14]

Signers of the second Manifesto include: sex experts
Sol Gordon and Albert Ellis, authors John Ciardi and
Isaac Asimov, Harvard psychologist B. F. Skinner (pio-
neer of behavioral modification), abortion activist
Allen F. Guttmacher, feminist Betty Friedan, and Rev.

Joseph Fletcher, the Episcopalian author of *Situation Ethics*.

The Unitarians helped in forming the American Humanist Association, which maintains a separate existence today, publishing its own journal of theology, *American Humanist*.

Some people realize the dangers of Secular Humanism, but few consider the extent of its influence through the spread of the historical-critical method through merger.

Apostasy through Merger

The history of the mainline churches in this century has been a record of institutional mergers and cooperative efforts Mergers have been sold to unsuspecting laity as great opportunities for saving money, increasing mission efforts, and working together more effectively. Instead, the result of *all* mainline mergers has been:

1) Doctrinal compromise,
2) Enormous expenditures of money,
3) A catastrophic loss of members and financial support,
4) Decades of bitter infighting among the merged factions.

Except for sex education, merger is the most oversold commodity in American life and the least effective in bringing about advertised results.

If mergers are so destructive to denominations, then why are they still being pursued with unrelenting zeal? The United Church of Christ is looking into merger with the Disciples of Christ. All the mainline groups are discussing union through the Consultation on Church Union. The real purpose of mainline merger is to absorb the assets of congregations, reduce confessional standards, and displace conservative leaders. All ecumenical endeavors serve to water down the scriptural basis for the church. Consider the results of these bridge-building efforts:

1. In Marxist-Christian dialogues, do the Marxists become more Christian, or do the Christians become more Marxist?
2. In Lutheran-Reformed talks, do the Lutherans convince the Calvinists about the Real Presence of the body and blood of Christ in the sacrament, or do the Reformed persuade the Lutherans to confuse the distinctions?
3. In Jewish-Christian discussions, do the Jews confess Jesus as the Messiah, or do the Christians admit that Judaism is sufficient without Christ?

Merger produces the same bitter fruit. When a somewhat more conservative denomination merges with a liberal group, the theology of the liberal group quickly dominates the new church body. The degenerative process is actually hastened by merger, since the obvious disparities of faith drive out the more conservative members and pastors, allowing the Left to whoop it up on their own.

When a denomination with property rights merges with another group where the congregation has no property rights, the effect of merger is to take away property rights from the conservatives, not to restore rights to the liberal group. The more liberal the denomination, the more tyrannical the rules concerning the ownership of property. In addition, newer congregations have even fewer rights than the older churches established in more democratic times.

Unionism
Hardly anyone believes that a group of Christians would allow the destructive effects of a merger based

upon losing property rights and giving up the inerrancy of Scripture, yet recent history shows how easily the worst can come about. Unionism is the best explanation for the development of destructive mergers. Unionism is the display of doctrinal unity through worship when agreement in faith does not exist. The term comes from the Prussian Church Union, 1830, which forced Lutheran and Reformed churches to unite with a common worship service without resolving major doctrinal differences, such as the Real Presence of the body and blood of Christ in Holy Communion and baptismal regeneration.

Confessions of faith must affirm the truths of Scripture but also reject false teaching. The Book of Concord clearly does both. However, the modern spirit of achieving institutional unity has degraded doctrinal clarity, not only among the mainline liberals, but also among the Evangelicals. Martin Reu, a seminary professor in the old American Lutheran Church, explained the problem of unionism:

> We find this attitude of tolerance quite frequently among unionists. It is often used to assuage a troubled conscience, one's own as well as that of others; for the unionist declares that everyone may continue to hold his own private convictions and merely needs to respect and tolerate those of another. This attitude is totally wrong, for it disregards two important factors: (a) In tolerating divergent doctrines one either denies the perspicuity and clarity of the Scriptures, or one grants to error the right to exist alongside of truth, or one evidences indifference over against biblical truth by surrendering its absolute validity; and (b) in allowing two opposite views concerning one doctrine to exist side by side, one has entered upon an inclined plane which of necessity leads ever further into complete doctrinal indifference, as may plainly be seen from

the most calamitous case on record, viz., the Prussian Union. Doctrinal indifference is at once the root of unionism and its fruit. Whoever accepts, in theory as well as in practice, the absolute authority of the Scriptures and their unambiguousness with reference to all fundamental doctrines, must be opposed to every form of unionism.[15]

In Lutheranism, the question of unionism has played a major role from the beginning. The first Lutheran church body in America, the General Synod, was founded to keep the congregations from joining with the Episcopalians. The Pennsylvania clergy reserved the right to withdraw from the General Synod, since they were thinking about merger with the Reformed. Later, when tensions grew between the revivalists on one side and the confessional Lutherans on the other side, the conservative General Council was formed in 1867 to bring about a confessional Lutheran church body in the East. By pulling out of the General Synod, the General Council deprived the General Synod of any resistance toward revivalism and the Social Gospel movement. Nevertheless, the General Council did not resolve some major doctrinal issues, such as pulpit and altar fellowship, the lodge, and the millenium.

When the General Synod and General Council reunited with the United Synod of the South, forming the United Lutheran Church in America in 1918, many doctrinal questions went unanswered. The inerrancy of Scripture was not an issue before the 1918 merger, but it soon became an issue for all Lutherans when the newly discovered historical-critical method began working into the seminaries. Liberal Lutherans continued to merge until the 1987 formation of the Evangelical Lutheran Church in

America, whose constitution avoids the clear doctrinal standards of the past, including the inerrancy of the Scriptures.

The doctrine of the mainline seminaries may be illustrated by selections from the dogmatics textbook which is used at all the seminaries of the Evangelical Lutheran Church in America, *Christian Dogmatics*.[16]

THE TRINITY

Truly, the Trinity is simply the Father and the man Jesus and their Spirit as the Spirit of the believing community. (I, p. 155)

THE INCARNATION, VIRGIN BIRTH, AND ASCENSION

The notion of the preexistent Son of God becoming a human being in the womb of a virgin and then returning to his heavenly home is bound up with a mythological picture of the world that clashes with our modern scientific world view. (I, p. 527)

The main statements of the Apostles' Creed are so bound up with its mythological form that to get rid of the myth would destroy the creed *in toto*. Can modern people still be expected to accept the creed, with its mythological elements? We know that in the scientific picture of the world, the categories "above" and "below" do not make sense. Therefore, the story of the descent of the Son of God to earth and his ascent into heaven cannot be taken literally. (I, p. 529)

THE MIRACLES

We must concede the possibility that miracles may have been attributed to people simply to enhance their status, that is, their special relationship to the gods. Each claim of truth must be carefully analyzed, and it should not be excluded that some of the miracles attributed to Jesus may have no historical basis and serve only to emphasize his exceptional status. (II, p. 283)

THE ATONEMENT

The one splattered against the front of our truck comes back to say "Shalom." There is no strange transaction that takes place somewhere in celestial bookkeeping halls to make it universal. (II, pp. 91-2)

Commenting on the Braaten-Jenson volumes, which he highly recommended, one ELCA pastor, considered a conservative, said, "They are a little weak in Christology."[17]

Merger Works

The greatest achievement of merger is in establishing the theology of the Unitarians. By making all things new, the denomination can eliminate troublesome confessional statements of the past, such as mischievous articles on the inerrancy of the Bible, the authority of previous confessions of faith, and fellowship principles. A new constitution can bypass such "outmoded" language and interject the philosophies of the Social Gospel, feminism, socialism, and the quota system. The new denomination can close down conservative pockets of resistance by fiat, erasing entire departments (the sober, diligent ones which built new congregations and engaged in some forms of modest evangelism) while funding new, "creative" efforts in institutional radicalism. Merger can also get rid of congregational constitutions which stipulate doctrinal standards for the minister and members.

Mainline Churches, Home Missions for the Unitarians

Visible Unitarians have fared poorly outside of New England, although they have been over-represented in positions of American leadership. However, Unitarians take great pride in the fact that the "green wood of Unitarianism has been grafted onto the old wood" of the mainline churches. F. E. Meyer noted: "As a liberal movement it has many spiritual brethren in the Reformed churches. As a result there are undoubtedly more Unitarians outside than inside the Unitarian fellowship." [18]

Unitarian theology developed from an overemphasis on the fatherhood of God among the Congregationalists and the euphoria felt over the new scientific age. Advocacy for the Social Gospel movement, delight in the theory of evolution, negative criticism of the Bible, and doctrinal liberalism were overlapping movements which gathered force in a united attack upon the Christian faith. At Yale, the integrity and authority of the Old Testament were under attack in the closing decades of the 19th century. In the opening decades of the 20th century, the divinity of Christ was denied.

Roman Catholics saw a similar decline develop later, since the Vatican opposed modern biblical criticism until after World War II. Now the head of the theology department of Notre Dame, Richard McBrien, routinely denounces the pope on national television, the department exults in its radical feminism, and Notre Dame's seminary teaches future priests that Jesus was a male chauvinist.[18]

The Unitarian process has completely overtaken the mainline denominations. The change has been slow but insidious. Many older clergy maintained some aspects of traditional Christianity while embracing the fatuousness of liberalism. The authority of the Scriptures became undermined when church leaders said the Bible was infallible in its doctrines but not in reporting historical, scientific, and geographical facts. Infallibility lost its original meaning by the 1930s, so some writers started using inerrancy to re-assert the original intent of the term infallibility. Now liberal church leaders assert that inerrancy is a new term, invented in the 1930s. A little truth can be very misleading.

History is never very simple or neat, but this is how denominations have turned away from their confessional standards over a period of time. The National Council of Churches denominations have completed these steps. Others, like the Southern Baptists and the Lutheran Church Missouri Synod, are pulling in three directions at once (conservative, charismatic, and liberal/Unitarian). Denial of historic Christianity has followed these successive steps in each denomination:

1. Old Testament narratives are no longer accepted as entirely accurate: the six-day creation, the creation of Adam and Eve, the Tower of Babel, the flood, the exodus. Science professors in the church-owned colleges are allowed to teach evolution as factual, Genesis as poetical.
2. Certain aspects of the life of Christ are questioned, following the methods used to undermine the authority and unity of the Old Testament.
3. A lot of noise is made about getting at the actual truth of what Christ said and did, separating that imaginary body of truth from traditional Christian doctrine.

4. A leading theologian discovers that Christ really wanted us to believe in political activism, not in him as Lord and Savior. Seminarians are urged to turn their denomination around.
5. Denominational leaders support pastors and professors on the "cutting edge," pleading with people to tolerate new ideas.
6. Anyone can question the central doctrines of the faith with impunity. If anything, apostates are rewarded and conservatives are punished in denominational promotions and perks.
7. Denominational funds are moved out of world missions and American missions, to fund political activism. Or the mission divisions retain the same names, but the work within them is changed from evangelism to radicalism, in the name of "reaching out with the gospel." One church official said piously, "Not one boy in our boys' home is a member of our church, so this institution is pure mission."
8. More and more clergy speak about the prophetic role of the denomination and denigrate such things as evangelism, worship, prayer, and home visitation.
9. Women are ordained without serious consideration of scriptural injunctions and centuries of practice.
10. Those who question the ordination of women can no longer obtain approval for ordination.
11. The denomination uses its name and funds to support abortion on demand, doing its best to hide this from most members.
12. Suddenly, a homosexual lobby appears in the denomination.
13. Charismatics grow in number as people struggle to recapture the vitality of the past or turn from corpse-cold liberalism.

Gradualism

Gradualism works well in slowly desensitizing people to the total impact of pretend-Christianity. A congregation may have a pastor who teaches the inerrancy of the Bible for 30 years. When he retires, after years of ignoring what the denomination has been doing, the congregation finds itself with pastoral candidates who waffle about every doctrinal question, who use weasel words to baffle the audience. At this point, people will not easily abandon the church building they have used for many years, the friends they have made. Worse, liberals in the congregation are supported by the denomination, and they unite behind the minister with a fuzzy theology. The congregation is divided. Ultimately, the crypto-Unitarians will win. The members most concerned about scriptural doctrine will join another congregation. Even if conservatives work together to install a conservative minister, the denomination will prevail in the future. Thus, the green wood of Unitarianism is grafted onto the old wood of the mainline denominations.

NOTES

1. *What Luther Says*, 8 vols., Grand Rapids: Baker Book House, I, p. 39.
2. Theodore Graebner, *The Lodge Examined by the Scriptures.* Jack Harris, *Freemasonry: The Invisible Cult in Our Midst,* Towson, Maryland: Jack Harris, 1983. Walter Martin, *The Maze of Mormonism,* Ventura: Regal Books, 1978. Walter Martin, *The Kingdom of the Cults,* Minneapolis: Bethany House Publishers, 1985. James R. Spencer, *Beyond Mormonism, An Elder's Story,* Old Tappan, NJ: Fleming H. Revell, 1984. Books and videotapes on the Masonic Lodge are available from John Ankerberg, P.O. Box 8977, Chattanooga, TN 37411.
3. March 7, 1988, page 1.
4. E. Michael Jones, "Requiem for a Liturgist: Endgame Dissent at Notre Dame," *Fidelity,* January, 1988. Jones has also published *Is Notre Dame Still Catholic?,* which treats the anti-Roman Catholic doctrine and practice of Notre Dame and her sister school St. Mary's. Jones was fired from St. Mary's for being pro-life.
5. Englewood Cliffs: Prentice-Hall, 1983, p. 150.
6. Michael Horton, ed., *The Agony of Deceit,* Chicago: Moody Bible Institute, 1990; cited in "Heresy on the Airwaves, A New Book Slams Televangelists for Doctrinal Errors," by Richard N. Ostling, *Time,* March 5, 1990, p. 62.
7. The Unitarians and Universalists merged in 1961 to form the UUA, acknowledging their common lack of faith. The Universalists have their own history up to 1961, but that story is not distinct enough to merit additional space here. One good way to remember the difference: the Unitarians taught that man was too good to be condemned to hell by God; the Universalists believed that God was too good to condemn man to hell. In either case, they neglected to check on what the Scriptures revealed.

   The Universalists tend to be more conservative on social issues than the Unitarians, so the Universalists might be included among those more conservative groups which have suffered from merger.
8. Debra Mason, "Unitarians Seek Bigger Role in U. S. Culture," *Columbus Dispatch*, October 31, p. 11A.
9. Sydney Ahlstrom, *A Religious History of America*, New Haven: Yale University Press, 1972. Ahlstrom's treatment of Unitarianism is rapturous.

10. The walkout of liberal Lutherans at Concordia Theological Seminary in St. Louis in 1974 was portrayed in apocalyptic terms by the press, who knew the liberal seminary president John Tietjen previously in his role as a public relations director for the Lutheran Council in the USA. What the media did not show was the return of the exiles for lunch, 20 minutes later, at the same school. Tietjen's role in history was assured when he quit after one month as ELCA's first Bishop of the Metro Chicago District.

11. David Robinson, *The Unitarians and the Universalists*,Westport: Greenwood Press, 1985, p. 144. When a Christian becomes a Unitarian, the U-U's call him a "come-outer," which sounds better than "apostate."

12. *Ibid.*, p. 146.

13. James Hitchcock, *What is Secular Humanism?* Ann Arbor: Servant Books, 1982, p. 11.

14. Ibid., p. 14.

15. M. Reu, *In the Interest of Lutheran Unity, Two Lectures*, Columbus: The Lutheran Book Concern, 1940, p. 20.

16. Carl Braaten, Robert Jenson, ed. *Christian Dogmatics, 2 vols.*, Philadelphia: Fortress Press, 1984.

17. *The Religious Bodies of America*, St. Louis: Concordia Publishing House, 1954, pp. 505f.

18. E. Michael Jones, *op. cit.*

3.

THE MAINLINE CHURCHES
AND EVOLUTION

Although many people assume that the greatest change in theology developed in the last 25 years, the great divide actually opened up in the 19th century. One is tempted to find a single cause, whether it be a growing acceptance of evolution or the historical-critical study of the Bible. However, the influences cannot be completely separated. One influence feeds on another. Increasing doubts about the Bible in the 1870s led to increasing faith in science and the new technology. The devastation of the Civil War in America gave way to an optimism about the progress of man. The United States began a period of economic and geographical expansion which did not abate until the reunification of Viet Nam in 1975.

In the last century, a gushy attitude toward science, combined with an optimism untainted by world war, caused intellectual leaders to embrace the theory of evolution with more enthusiasm and certainty than Charles Darwin displayed in proposing it. Although the theory of evolution had been put forward in various forms before Darwin, the 1859 publication of *The*

Origin of Species by Means of Natural Selection or the Preservation of Favoured Races in the Struggle for Life, based upon Darwin's 1831 voyage on the *Beagle,* caused a sensation which continues to this day. Briefly, the theory of evolution assumes gradual and beneficial changes in organisms over a vast period of time. Some theorists claim that everything came about by chance and natural mechanisms, while others argue for some role by God in evolution.

The Social Gospel movement thrived in the same environment as evolution, promoting the same uncritical attitude about the potential of man and the same critical attitude toward the Scriptures. In some cases, evolutionary thought and Social Gospel enthusiasm coalesced. Washington Gladden (1836-1918), an early Social Gospel leader who ministered in Columbus, Ohio, popularized the new attitude toward the Bible in *Who Wrote the Bible?*, 1894. According to Richard Hofstadter, intellectual historian:

> The rise of biblical criticism and comparative religion the general relaxation of fundamentalist faith encouraged by the liberal clergy, prepared many Americans for the acceptance of Darwinism. James Freeman Clarke's *Ten Great Religions*, a liberal study of world creeds, ran through twenty-two editions in the fifteen years after its first appearance in 1871.[1]

Some religious leaders resisted the new enthusiasm for evolution. J. B. Reimensnyder, a Lutheran seminary professor, wrote *The Six Days of Creation; the Fall; and the Deluge* in 1886. Reimensnyder declared in his preface:

> The first chapter of the Bible—the sublimest ever penned—in such few words settling the greatest questions respecting God, Creation, the

World, and Man, has of late been made the special target for skeptical attacks. These assaults, sometimes from an open infidel, and sometimes from a Judas in ministerial garb, have been clothed in popular form and sensational dress, and circulated far and wide, sowing the seeds of incalculable moral mischief.[2]

Theodore Graebner (1876-1950), professor at Concordia Seminary in St. Louis, published *Essays on Evolution* in 1925 in the wake of the sensational Scopes Monkey trial in Dayton, Tennessee, where teacher John Scopes went on trial for violating the Tennessee Anti-Evolution Law, was found guilty, but was fined only $100. Graebner wrote that the Associated Press, after the trial ended, falsely reported a Lutheran being excommunicated in Kendallville, Indiana, for growing hybrid gladioli, a violation of the divine plan. The excommunicated Lutheran was not a Lutheran, not a member of the church in question, and not a resident of the neighborhood for at least 18 years.[3] Such were the passions kindled 65 years after the publication of *The Origin of the Species.*

Harvard, Yale, and Princeton, known for theological leadership among the mainline denominations, prepared the way for Darwin's acceptance in America. The 1869 appointment of Charles William Elliot, a chemist, as president of Harvard, marked the beginning of an emphasis on science and a new tolerance for unorthodox thought. At Yale, President Noah Porter accommodated himself to evolution in 1877, impressed by the fossil collection of Yale Professor Marsh at the campus's Peabody Museum. At Princeton, President James McCosh gave a qualified endorsement of Darwinism already in 1871, long before the Fundamentalist controversy of the 1920s.[4]

Thomas Huxley, called "Darwin's Bulldog," was invited to address the 1876 opening of Johns Hopkins

University in Baltimore, Maryland, an institution that has remained in the forefront of scientific research. The British scientist found himself lionized by the American press but lambasted by the clergy. Clearly, evolution was the newest trend of the new scientific age, with a vast and continuing influence on American thought. Henry Adams wrote about himself in the aftermath of the Civil War:

> He felt, like nine men in ten, an instinctive belief in Evolution . . . Natural Selection led back to Natural Evolution, and at last to Natural Uniformity. This was a vast stride. Unbroken Evolution under uniform conditions pleased everyone except curates and bishops; it was the very best substitute for religion; a safe, conservative, practical, thoroughly Common-Law deity.[5]

Many found it easy to identify evolution with the best and brightest in America, the promise of tomorrow, while connecting creation with the oppressive and stultifying forces of the past.

Henry Ward Beecher and his successor, Lyman Abbott, supported evolution. Both exerted considerable influence upon American thought. Beecher called himself a "cordial Christian evolutionist."[6] Abbott wrote *The Theology of an Evolutionist* in 1897. The "scientific" study of the Bible was embraced by a growing body of European professors, who trained many of the leading American theology professors, like Walter Rauschenbusch. The Industrial Revolution, unleashed by the new technology, built up a record of gross abuses of human rights in that century. Charles Darwin and Herbert Spencer provided a philosophy which appealed not only to the wealthy, but also to social reformers and to Karl Marx.

Thus, the mainline attitude toward evolution and Genesis was determined already in the 19th century.

The Social Gospel movement grew and spread during the last decades of the 19th century, closely allied with liberal, optimistic theology and the new biblical criticism from Europe. By 1900 Yale Divinity School was teaching the historical-critical method. It was very appealing, in the name of scientific study of the Bible, to think that Genesis was the work of several inconsistent authors, that the mighty acts of God were in fact myths conveying universal truths.

Leaders of the Social Gospel movement were Washington Gladden ("O Master, Let Me Walk with Thee"), Frank Mason North ("Where Cross the Crowded Ways of Life"), Harry Emerson Fosdick, and Walter Rauschenbusch (*A Theology for the Social Gospel,* 1917). North helped write the Social Creed of the Methodist Church, 1908.

The Federal Council of Churches was formed as the institutional wing of the Social Gospel movement and used virtually the same creed. The National Council of Churches is a direct descendant of the Federal Council. Rauschenbusch had the greatest impact in the group both as writer and teacher, with phenomenal popular success during his lifetime and continued appeal thereafter. The Social Gospel movement spread through the dedicated work of The Brotherhood of the Kingdom, an elite group which met year after year to promote a revolution in the church.[7]

The new theology of that era is easy to describe, even easier to learn. Nothing divine in the Bible can be taken at face value. All the miracles have natural explanations, including the virgin birth of Christ. Jesus was simply an outstanding rabbi who taught the Brotherhood of Man and the Fatherhood of God. Somehow Paul and the others imagined that Jesus was the Son of God and in all good faith invented appropriate myths about him. The real truth of Christianity, they argued, was that men should bring about the Kingdom of God (a key term for all Social Gospel leaders) through social reforms: child labor legislation, laws to legalize unions, old age pensions, pure food and drug regulation, and peace agreements.

The old doctrinal terms were maintained, but the meaning of those terms was distorted to convey the substance of liberal, man-centered optimism. Rauschenbusch's *Theology for the Social Gospel* is an excellent example of this approach, similar in many respects to Adolph Harnack's *What is Christianity?*, 1901.

Rauschenbusch penned these lines in *Christianizing the Social Order,* showing the same schoolboy enthusiasm for evolution as Henry Adams did in his autobiography:

> Translate the evolutionary theories into religious faith, and you have the doctrine of the Kingdom of God. This combination with scientific evolutionary thought has freed the kingdom ideal of its catastrophic setting and its background of demonism, and so adapted it to the climate of the modern world.[8]

One can hardly convey the childish enthusiasm with which these leaders greeted the newest insights of European scholars. They felt liberated, enlightened, propelled by inexorable Fate toward a man-made paradise. Mainline church leaders were joined by industrial giants in the New Faith. After reading Darwin and Spencer, Andrew Carnegie, the steel monopolist, intoned:

> I remember that light came as in a flood and all was clear. Not only had I got rid of theology and the supernatural, but I had found the truth of evolution. 'All is well since all grows better,' became my motto, my true source of comfort. Man was not created with an instinct for his own degradation, but from the lower he had

risen to the higher forms. Nor is there any conceivable end to his march to perfection. His face is turned to the light; he stands in the sun and looks upward.[9]

Looking at his old domain, Carnegie would now see the Rust Bowl, a symbol of the steel industry's continuing endurance and progress.

Another person with enormous influence and bottomless pockets for exerting power was oil baron John D. Rockefeller. His efforts to create a liberal Protestant cartel through the Interchurch Movement collapsed in 1920, but the building still serves Social Gospel heirs as headquarters for the National Council of Churches and the American branch of the World Council of Churches, 475 Riverside Drive, New York City.

Rockefeller rescued Harry Emerson Fosdick from possible unemployment and installed him at the Rockefeller-funded Riverside Church in New York City. Fosdick published the famous article, "Shall the Fundamentalists Win?" in 1922 in *Christian Century*, leading to his position at Riverside Church. He was decidedly in favor of evolution.[10] Considering the impact of Carnegie and Rockefeller funding, the leadership of Fosdick, Rauschenbusch, and their heirs, the marvel is that anyone in Christendom accepts the biblical account of creation as revealed in the word of God.

The Catholic Church has been influenced through the paleontologist Pierre Teilhard de Chardin, S.J., in *The Phenomenon of Man,* an evolutionist tract once banned by the Vatican. In 1895, Father John Zahm of Notre Dame wrote a book in favor of evolution, banned at the time by the Vatican. Etienne Gilson, a highly regarded Aquinas scholar, and Karl Rahner, a prolific author, have both made evolution more acceptable to Catholics. The New Baltimore Catechism allowed for theistic evolution, just as Protestant apologists allowed for biblical accounts subordinated to current theories.

Teaching a modified form of evolution was allowed by the papal encyclical *Humani generis,* 1950. According to one evolutionist author, the effect of Rome's stringent measures against modernism was "to delay the Church's accommodation to evolutionary biology and biblical scholarship."[11]

When there are court cases about allowing the theory of evolution to be criticized in public school, the mainline churches file briefs along with the American Civil Liberties Union against the teaching of creation. Mainline church leaders do not consider opposing the biblical account of creation a matter of censorship but an issue of protecting innocent children from the imposition of religious views. For others, the Bible remains completely true, able to withstand the hammer blows of the most savage attacks. A Lutheran would rather stand on one word of the Bible than join the world in attacking it.

Another Approach to Evolution

"Darwin" is carved over the west portal of Riverside Church, the symbol of mainline religion and the influence of the Social Gospel movement. For some believers, Darwin is the very symbol of the Antichrist, the source of everything evil in society today. In their zeal to defend the faith, they have often tried to portray Darwin as a poor scientist with no qualifications. Or they have shown how absurd the early statements about evolution appear to the average Christian of today, forgetting that equally foolish statements from Christians in the past do not constitute a devastating argument against the Word of God. If Darwin's reputation were destroyed tomorrow, his influence would remain.

Many of us find ourselves in a peculiar situation today, able to see the basic flaws in evolution, but lacking the scientific training to examine closely the claims of science. As Dr. Paul Boehlke of Dr. Martin Luther

College has written, if we place our trust in a particular proof of scriptural truth, such as Noah's Ark, or the Shroud, or human footprints among dinosaur tracks, we will be devastated when the evidence evaporates. Using reason to assist the claims of the Word of God is clearly a Reformed approach to the Scriptures, one which threatens the gospel itself, even though the motives seem worthwhile.[12]

Furthermore, the typical layman or pastor cannot discuss evolution on the same level as a scientist with a Ph.D. and years of research, whose journals and textbooks assume evolution. A frontal attack might be met with such questions as this: "And where did you read this?" or "Have you earned a degree in biology, chemistry, or physics?" The authors who defend creation are not taken seriously by scientists, who may not wish to have their concept of reality challenged by a dabbler in the field. Many scientists understand such confrontations to be reminiscent of the Dark Ages, when teaching the earth to be the center of the universe was a measure of one's orthodoxy. Galileo (1564-1642), they remember from History of Science 101, was forced by the Vatican to recant his theories, which were correct.

Darwin, Theologian and Scientist

The popular image of Charles Darwin as a fire-breathing revolutionary is hardly fair. He grew up well-to-do as the child of a physician, showing a great deal of interest in insects as a child. Medical school at Edinburgh did not hold his interest, so his father sent him to Cambridge to study theology. One religious television expert, who tried to claim that Darwin's only formal training was in theology, evidently did not realize that the Cambridge student befriended two of the dominant men of science in Britain at the time, engaging them in long conversations. One can hardly fault Darwin as having lack of training in science or even as being prejudiced against creation His professors belonged to the old school which did not assume an antagonism between science and faith.

When Darwin left Cambridge, he still believed in the "strict and literal truth of every word in the Bible. . . ."[13]

The effect of Darwin's theory was a natural eroding of religious faith, since human reason made "natural causes" more appealing to the new scientific mind than the hand of God. Darwin's wife touched upon the issue in a letter to him which still expresses today what many believers would say about evolution:

> It seems to me also that the line of your pursuits may have led you to view chiefly the difficulties on one side, and that you have not had time to consider and study the chain of difficulties on the other; but I believe you do not consider your opinion as formed.
>
> May not the habit in scientific pursuits of believing nothing till it is proved, influence your mind too much in other things which cannot be proved in the same way, and which if true, are likely to be above our comprehension?

Darwin wrote at the end of this letter: "When I am dead, know that many times I have kissed and cried over this. C. D."[14]

The Earthworm, Darwin's Nemesis

Shortly after his voyage on the *Beagle* was over, Darwin began a study of earthworms which continued until 1881, when he published *The Formation of Vegetable Mould Through the Action of Worms With Observations on their Habits.* Darwin died in 1882.

Darwin's earthworm book is so thorough in its observations that no one has ventured to improve upon it.

The Earthworm Book stated:

Darwin is remembered chiefly for his classic works, *The Origin of Species* and *The Descent of Man,* two books that have never ceased to stir controversy, particularly in religious circles. Yet in its importance to agriculture and human nutrition—and thus human welfare—his modest volume on earthworms may well, in the final analysis, be his greatest work.[15]

Although Darwin neglected the application of his research for agriculture, his observations, combined with our new appreciation for the environment, point us toward the opposite conclusion of his first research. For that reason, the earthworm, the object of 44 years of observation, is Darwin's nemesis.

Purpose

A scientist can observe, measure, and propose theories, but he cannot answer one basic question: that of purpose.

The beginning may fascinate everyone. How did this come about? But the ultimate question still revolves around purpose. We all know that the bee needs the blossom, and the blossom the bee. But why do they work together, toward what end?

If we look at the interdependence of nature, something we can observe in our own backyards, we can see a multitude of relationships, not only between one creature and another, but among all the creatures and plants together, along with the ever-changing elements of the weather and soil. While man-made businesses fail and powerful empires collapse, in spite of their power, energy, and efficiency, the natural world thrives without the wisdom of man, and suffers because of it. If one can envision an empire and build it, as did Alexander, Ghengis Khan, and Stalin, then one vast creative power must be the source of the organization of the natural world.

For some people, science is intimidating. They think of giant telescopes silently following the stars, taking measurements which only astrophysicists can discuss. They picture analytical chemistry labs, filled with mass spectrometers, gas chromatograms, electron microscopes,and nuclear reactors. They consider the light-speed calculations of computers and conclude, "I could never be a scientist."

Not knowing how awesome science might become, Solomon wrote, through the Holy Spirit, on the basis of his backyard observations:

> Go to the ant, O sluggard; consider her ways and be wise. Without having any chief, officer or ruler, she prepares her food in summer, and gathers her sustenance in harvest.(Proverbs 6:6-8 RSV)

In the same way, we can look at one small corner of the universe and draw conclusions, without elaborate and expensive instruments, government grants, or graduate assistants. Our own backyards are a natural science laboratory.

Earthworms belong to the phylum of invertebrates known as Annelida, named for the rings of muscles (*annellus,* Latin for ring) which characterize them. The bristles that help propel earthworms through the soil earn them the title of Oligochaeta, or those bristle-footed worms with only a few bristles. Most earthworms belong to the genus *Lumbricus* and are called lumbricids. About 1800 species of earthworms are known to exist. The most common in the backyard are the nightcrawler *(L. terrestris)*, the manure worm *(Eisenia foetida),* the red wiggler *(L. rubellus)*, and the field worm *(Allolobophora caliginosa)*. The Australians have a species of earthworm which is over four feet long.

The worm has been so much a symbol of lowliness that hymns stressing humility are called vermicular, from the Latin word for worm. The Bible calls man a worm in Job 25:6, and the Savior is compared to a worm in Psalm 22:6. But some hymns went too far:

Oh, may Thy powerful Word inspire this feeble worm.
To rush into Thy kingdom, Lord, and take it as by storm.
                    and

Worms, strike your harps, your voices tune,
And warble forth your lays;
Leap from the earth with pious mirth
To trumpet forth your praise.[16]

First of all, the earthworm is a creature of the soil, tunneling through all varieties with the greatest of ease, a talent we take for granted until the benefits of this tunneling becomes more obvious to us. The earthworm is nothing more than a tiny hydraulic drill, using its hard, pointed prostomium to probe through soil, its mouth to swallow whatever cannot be pushed aside, its bristles and rings of muscles and intestinal pressure to worm its way through the toughest barriers. One woman put asphalt around her garage to promote drainage, only to find the tar riddled with worm holes, time after time.

The burrowing of the earthworm has a number of positive effects on the soil. The first and most obvious benefit is mixing the soil. Darwin has shown that earthworms bring soil up to the surface in their castings (excrement). All layers of soil are mixed gradually, though not completely. Many high-tech gardeners scoff at the tiny bit of soil moved by an earthworm in one day, about equal to its body weight. Unlike the gardener, though, the earthworm works continuously, without any tools, being careful to leave plants and delicate roots undisturbed The loosening effect promotes plant growth, because plants do not grow in soil but between soil particles. The most certain way to eliminate all plant growth is to walk on it daily. Soil compaction will quickly kill the roots. Footpaths are killing zones for earthworms and plant roots.

Compacted soil will not recover quickly, unless an organic covering is provided to entice earthworms back to that area. A layer of dead grass, leaves, or manure on a compacted footpath will promote earthworm activity, make the soil springy again, and promote growth.

Earthworms work in the upper twelve inches of the soil, where almost all plant life sends its roots. Even trees do most of their feeding in the top layer, called the rhizozone. Tunneling provides a number of other benefits worth considering, all essential to productive soil: aeration of the soil, infiltration of water, humification, and fertilization.

Soil without air is called a bog, noted for its bad smell and exotic plants. But unless one raises skunk cabbages, which grow only in a bog, unaerated soil is not desirable. The earthworm constantly opens up channels for air to penetrate the soil, encouraging healthy bacteria and molds to grow, promoting the constant decaying process which feeds all living things.

Infiltration of water increases as earthworms open up channels for water to penetrate. People with clay soil will see round worm holes dotting the surface. Earthworms decrease erosion by making the soil more spongelike. Instead of holding the water on the surface, the channels let the water percolate down rather than wash away with the finest and best soil particles. The more earthworms, the greater the rate of percolation. Clay soil supports a greater number of earthworms than sandy soil. Clay also needs the percolating effect of the tunnels.

The tunneling habits of earthworms improve the soil in two other ways mentioned above. First of all, worms pull organic material down into the tunnels for food.

Secondly, they leave their castings in the tunnels and on the soil surface. Both habits, to be treated subsequently, add to the fertility and water retention of the soil. No gardener could improve so much soil with such meticulous care. God can and does renew the soil in time, but man in his haste to produce has often destroyed the virgin land which once produced so abundantly without him.

The earthworm excels in the arena of feeding. Not only is the feeding itself valuable, since it removes dead organic material from the surface of the soil, but the final product of feeding, the cast, is also valuable. The earthworm itself is little more than mouth, stomach, and intestine. Food, which can be soil or humus material (leaves, manure, dead grass), enters the earthworm through the prostomium at the anterior. In the pharynx, food starts to break down through mixing, moistening, and secretions (amylase, and from the calciferous glands, calcium carbonate). The calciferous glands seem to regulate pH for the earthworm, which cannot abide acid soil. The earthworms neutralize acid soil for their own benefit and thereby increase soil productivity. This liming or sweetening effect releases other soil chemicals for plants to use.[17]

The crop of the earthworm stores food until it is ground up in the muscular gizzard. Soil particles and very small bits of stone serve as abrasive material to grind up tough materials In the process, soil particles and small stones are ground finer than before, as Darwin pointed out. Fine particles are easily lost through water and wind erosion, so they need to be replaced. Food leaves the gizzard and enters the intestine, which continues the digestive process. The earthworm excretes solid material castings from its anus and nitrogenous liquid through its nephridia (a simple form of kidneys). Earthworm mucus adds nitrogen to the soil.

The end result of earthworm feeding makes the soil better, for a number of reasons. The earthworm is a "colloid mill," a small chemical plant which produces an array of chemicals, and concentrates other chemicals in its castings, mucus, and nephridia excretions. It increases the bacterial count in the soil and breaks down humus material in its castings. Earthworms may seem insignificant, weighing only 1/30 of an ounce, but they are the most abundant, active, and beneficial of the higher soil creatures. Ants tunnel, aerate, and even humify the soil to a great degree; they are indeed the hardworking undertakers of the insect world, carrying off corpses in solemn processions. Still, earthworms are never harmful pests, as ants often are, and earthworms do not have the disgusting trait of protecting and caring for other pests (as ants do for aphids). Nor do earthworms get into the house.

The final benefit of the earthworm's contribution is realized when the creature dies. The earthworm's dry weight is 72% protein, which is largely nitrogen, an essential component of all plant life. According to Lawrence and Millar, 70% of worm protein is available to plants two weeks after the creature's death. The slow release of nitrogen, advertised in commercial fertilizer, is the earthworm's life and death, for free.

A British minister noted once that earthworms "are much addicted to venery," so we can count on them to increase and multiply. They thrive in moist conditions, so spring and autumn rains boost their population. Lawns and gardens support a large population of earthworms, and the earthworms support a large population of robins, who thrive on worms.

Likewise, rabbits devour high nitrogen food, such as grass and clover, leaving copious droppings high in nitrogen, which feed the earthworm population, which promote the growth of high nitrogen plants, such as grass and clover.

Compost

If the earthworm alone seems to be a marvel of simple complexity, then the compost pile is a global corporation involving millions of clients. Once again, the earthworm plays a role.

The compost pile is an ancient concept which was adapted by Sir Albert Howard for use in India, then imported to America through the influence of organic gardening methods. The compost pile (or pit) is made up of layers of soil and organic material. The piles are kept moist, shaded, and aerated. *National Geographic* offers an excellent photo expedition into "The Wild World of Compost," by Cecil Johnson.[18]

This is how one compost pile progressed. Wire fencing was formed into a circle five feet in diameter in the shade of three trees. The base was bare soil, allowing easy access to earthworms, who rush in at the end to celebrate the finish of composting. Grass clippings, leaves, weeds, and soil were placed in layers in the pile, about four feet high. The wire fence allowed air to reach the pile. The pile was hosed down every week and stirred somewhat for several months. All extra weeds and grass clipping were added to the top. Some rabbit manure was also added.

Composting requires high nitrogen materials, grass as opposed to tree leaves, to create the first stage of the rotting process. Thermophilic or heat-loving bacteria act first, releasing heat as they attack organic material high in nitrogen. The temperature of the pile may reach 170 degrees Fahrenheit. Even a bag of grass clippings left alone will heat up. Earthworms would melt during this stage of decomposition, so they stay away.

When the pile cools down, many things happen at once. Fungus starts to form, attacking plant structures with their filaments. Bacteria continue to work, joined by the earthy-smelling actinomycetes in the soil. Millions and millions of springtails, a tiny insect, feed upon fungi and organic matter. Mites, millipedes, centipedes, and sowbugs join the corporate effort. The higher level creatures feed on the lower level creatures, the biomass teeming with life and death, reproduction and destruction. No matter where the pile is formed, if the raw materials are present, the decomposition team will arrive and reduce the pile to the basic elements needed by plant life, shrinking it in the process.

When the compost has been recycled through millions of creatures, the earthworm begins a steady trip to the top of the heap. Shunning both heat and light, the earthworm will invade no pile before its time. As the most complex of the processing units, the earthworm requires that much of the work be done first. Some of the workers will gladly dine on earthworms, but the earthworms consume only the semi-rotted material, making it even more useful for plants.

Like any other creature when given ideal conditions, the earthworm will reproduce with wild abandon in the dark moistness of compost. The egg capsules they form as the result of their mating provide a fairly strong vehicle for even more earthworms when the compost is distributed. The pile of weeds, clippings, and garbage is converted into the richest form of soil, soil chemicals stabilized in the forms most usable to plants, unborn earthworms in egg capsules poised for work at the first rain.

The rotting process binds sandy soil together, loosens clay, and breaks down humus to be used again in a new crop. Compost holds water better than a sponge. Disease pathogens are killed by the various battles within the pile. John Greenleaf Whittier even wrote a poem about the sanitizing effect of the soil's natural process.

The compost pile seems to be a banquet for the entire animal kingdom. Birds gather to snatch fat bugs and worms from the top of the pile. Moles burrow underneath to reach the riotous mass of earthworms working their way upward through the pile. Cats and hawks gather to dine on the birds. Rabbits nibble at the greens fed by the compost pile. The chickaree squirrel curses at everyone, angry and never tired of loudly displaying his ill humor.

To test the benefits of compost, the author dug a pit four feet deep, six feet long, and four feet wide. Truthfully, neighborhood children dug the pit, fueled by promises of all the ice cream they could hold. The pit was filled for the winter with newsprint, the Christmas tree, brush, garbage, grass clippings, manure, soil, and weeds. In the spring the area was planted with Silver Queen corn, Kentucky Wonder pole beans (which grew up the corn stalks), and Atlantic Giant pumpkins. Gourds volunteered from the compost.

An agriculture expert from Dow Chemical, who loved to raise corn, visited the plot, to see whose Silver Queen was higher. His face filled with awe as he followed the green stalks up to the peak of the garage, which first hid them from his view. "Silver Queen is a short variety. It isn't supposed to grow nine feet tall!" He expressed the fear or hope that the giant ears were overgrown and bad tasting, only to be disappointed. The corn brought its share of critters, from the birds looking for earthworms to the neighbors whose conversation gravitated consistently to the good old days when they grew sweet corn and ate it fresh. Since the earthworm and his friends did almost all the work, the garden easily fed the neighborhood, provided for Halloween, put gourds on many tables, and offered fresh beans for children to snack on.

Why?

People who have tried to organize an event with volunteers know how difficult it can be to find a group of people who will work together for a common purpose and accomplish a task successfully in a given amount of time. If the compost pile got attacked the way most human problems are solved, human life would not survive the ensuing chaos in nature. Not only is each creature uniquely suited to his role, but all living things work together toward improving the environment. No one is late. No one is too proud to do the most disgusting and lowly work. No one gets tired or bored. No one lords it over the rest, but all work together in humble servitude.

Since intelligent life has so much trouble getting through the routine tasks, the interdependence of all life, with man at the apex, forces the question of purpose. Our poor designs and flawed execution compel us to say of each and every creature, "I see the hand of the Creator in every aspect of nature."

For the believer who confronts the unbelieving scientist, the solution is not in proving to him that the compost pile works better than the United Nations, but in asking him why it is so. The interdependence requires design rather than random chance, and the question of purpose transcends the normal scientific quest.

For the Believer

The Christian has only one miracle to grasp, one continuing wonder—that God became man. No one can explain the mystery, which is revealed through faith. That God's own Son died on the cross for the sins of the world must be a part of the continuing wonder. The cross and God becoming man are the same theme, a unity which places in perspective all other wonders in the universe, each of which reflects the light of the Word Incarnate.

A Lutheran pastor who could not believe that God created the world in six days posed an enigma for himself. He believed that the Bible is completely true, without any errors or contradictions. He accepted the Lutheran confessions as genuine interpretations of Scripture. Therefore, he had to believe that God became man, and what truth is more difficult to continue to hold in this age of man becoming god? Therefore, if

God became man and lived among us, full of grace and truth, then what weakness did He once have, which prevented him from creating the universe in six days rather than six billion years? Or walking on water? Or changing water into wine? Or feeding us with his body and blood until the day of his coming?

Mainline Malaise

The catastrophic decline of the mainline churches has been preceded by a retreat from the revealed doctrine of creation. Mainline malaise did not begin with doubting the divinity of Christ but with qualifying the creation and the historicity of Adam and Eve. At first, already in the 19th century, Christian leaders who might be called conservative today started accommodating themselves to the theory of evolution. Their mistake was manifold. First of all, they chose a current mode of thought over an eternal truth in the interest of being part of the current trend. The science of each era soon becomes obsolete, even comical. Some remember being taught that the universe consisted of one galaxy, ours, and that we lived in the middle of it. Now thousands of galaxies are clearly recorded on photographic film. Larger telescopes changed astrophysics, but not the Word of God.

Another error of accommodation manifested itself years later. The spirit of trendiness replaced a "Christian evolution" with evolution itself, effectively denying purpose for man and the universe, giving aid and comfort to the Enemy by undermining all the doctrines of the Word of God.

The subtlest error of accommodation is still being practiced today, by those who believe they oppose compromise. By offering a reasonable explanation for revealed doctrine which transcends reason, something which even Darwin's wife doubted possible, they are setting the stage for new accommodation. While it is a service to describe the chemical complexities of the bombadier beetle, believers are hardly served by scientists clamoring to prove an article of faith with physical evidence. This is the spirit of rationalism, a thirst which will not be sated by more brine.

Creation

The explanation for the First Article of the Creed in Luther's Small Catechism is rather simple:

> I believe that God has created me and all that exists; that He has given me and still sustains my body and soul, all my limbs and senses, my reason and all the faculties of my mind, together with food and clothing, house and home, family and property; that He provides me daily and abundantly with all the necessities of life, protects me from all danger, and preserves me from all evil.

Luther was able to answer why this has taken place:

> All this He does out of His pure, fatherly, and divine goodness and mercy, without any merit or worthiness on my part. For all of this I am bound to thank, praise, serve and obey Him.

Rather than pontificate about the "god-like ability of the mind to refashion the world," a popular concept in current self-help courses and cults, Luther taught the centrality of God's mercy and love, not only in providing for us, but also in saving us. Our purpose is to love and serve, thank, praise, and obey him.

The spirit of enthusiasm has been with us from the beginning, ever since Adam and Eve trusted their feelings instead of the word of God. That same spirit of enthusiasm permeates the leadership of mainline churches, who upon forsaking the genuine Redeemer, have pursued the goal of redeeming the world for themselves. The recent *Lutheran Book of Worship* even contains a prayer for each setting of Holy Communion where the people pledge themselves to the redemption of the world. The spirit of enthusiasm, therefore, is man-centered rather than God-centered. Evolution has fueled this unwarranted optimism, not only in the Social Gospel movement, but also in the social sciences which have been allies in activism: social work, psychology, and education.[19]

The results of evolutionary thought on our society can be found in every area of social concern, from the destruction of helpless unborn babies to the health and wealth messages of pseudo-Christian teachers. Thinking it odd and humiliating to "bend the knee, while we own the mystery," man instead worships his own progress, his own goals, and his own body.

God reveals himself in nature only to a limited degree, showing his infinite power, architectural genius, and organizational skill.

> For the anger of God is being revealed from heaven against all the ungodliness and unrighteousness of people who suppress the truth by their unrighteousness. What can be known about God is clear to them, because God has made it clear to them. For since the creation of the world, they have seen the unseen things of God. From the things He created, they can tell that He has everlasting power and is God. Therefore they have no excuse, since they knew God but did not honor Him as God, nor did they thank Him. Instead, their thoughts became total nonsense, and their ignorant hearts were darkened. (Romans 1:18-21 NET)

Against the me-centered message favored by men, Paul placed the Christ-centered message of the gospel.

> So if anyone is in Christ, he is a new creation. The old things have passed away; they have become new! But God has done it all. He reconciled us to Himself, through Christ, and gave us the responsibility of distributing this reconciliation. (2 Corinthians 5:17,18 NET)

Because God has done all this for us, apart from any merit or virtue on our part, our thankfulness is expressed in deeds of kindness for our neighbor.

> Yes, by His grace you are saved through faith. It was not your own doing; it is God's gift. It is not the result of anything you have done; and so no one may boast. For He has made us what we are, creating us in Christ Jesus to do good works, which God prepared in advance for us to do. (Ephesians 2:8-10 NET)

Such a message is quite the opposite in origin and purpose of the once popular self-help gospel: "Every day in every way I am getting better and better."

Devolution

Darwin began his lifelong study of earthworms to understand how boulders and ancient buildings slowly disappeared beneath the level of the soil. He concluded his study with this statement: "It may be doubted whether there are many other animals which have played so important a part in the history of the world, as have these lowly organized creatures."[20] His study showed that all the monuments of man's ingenuity, no matter how great, would inevitably be covered up by the relentless tunneling of worms, who add 1/4 inch of soil each year.

For those who have seen the power of God, whether in the fierce and glowing magma of the volcano or the tender love of the mother robin, the earthworm's purpose is clearly part of God's plan to care for us. The Christian life is often described most eloquently in great hymns:

> Yea, Lord, 'twas thy rich bounty gave
> My body, soul, and all I have
> In this poor life of labor.
> Lord, grant that I in every place
> May glorify Thy lavish grace
> And serve and help my neighbor.
> Let no false doctrine me beguile,
> Let Satan not my soul defile.
> Give strength and patience unto me
> To bear my cross and follow Thee.
> Lord Jesus Christ,
> My God and Lord, My God and Lord,
> In death Thy comfort still afford.
> (*The Lutheran Hymnal,* 429)

But there is no Christian life without returning to the Author of Life, who guides and nourishes us with his word and sacrament.

NOTES

1. *Social Darwinism in American Thought,* Boston: Beacon Press, 1955, pp. 14f.
2. Philadelphia: Lutheran Publication Society, p. iii.
3. St. Louis: Concordia Publishing House. p. 5.
4. Hofstadter, *op. cit.,* p. 19.
5. *Ibid*, pp. 15f; citing *The Education of Henry Adams,* New York: Modern Library, 1931, pp. 225-6.
6. *Ibid*, p. 29.
7. Frederic M. Hudson, "The Reign of the New Humanity: A Study of the Background, History and Influence of the Brotherhood of the Kingdom." Unpublished doctoral dissertation, Columbia University, 1968.
8. *Christianizing the Social Order,* p. 9. Cited in: Hofstadter, *op. cit.* p.108.
9. Andrew Carnegie, *Autobiography,* Boston, 1920, quoted in Hofstadter, op. cit., p. 45.
10. Fosdick is listed as a modern-day prophet in the text of the Lutheran Church in America's *Word and Witness* program. The author of the chapter, Philadelphia Seminary professor John Reumann, was on the Commission for a New Lutheran Church. A Seminex contribution to the debate over evolution is William A. Schmeling, *Creation versus Evolution? NOT REALLY!* St. Louis: Clayton Publishing House, 1976.
11. John C. Green, *Darwin and the Modern World View,* (Baton Rouge: Louisiana State University Press, 1961), p. 17. *Darwinism and Divinity ,* ed. by John Durant; Basil Blackwell, London, 1985. A popular treatment of the scientific problems involved in evolution can be found in Luther D. Sunderland, *Darwin's Enigma: Fossils and Other Problems,* Santee, California: Master Book Publishers, 1988.
12. Paul R. Boehlke, "The Bible and Science," unpublished paper delivered at Concordia College, River Forest, Illinois, June, 1980. "The Nature and Teaching of Science in Lutheran Schools," unpublished paper delivered at New Ulm, Minnesota, March, 1989.
13. F. Darwin, (1888) ed. *The Life and Letters of Charles Darwin, 3 vols.,* London: John Murray, I, p. 146. Cited in Michael Denton, *Evolution: A Theory in Crisis,* Bethesda: Adler and Adler, 1985, p. 25.
14. N. Barlow, (1958) *Autobiography of Charles Darwin,* London: Collins, pp. 235-7; cited in Denton, op. cit., pp. 54f.
15. Jerry Minnich, *The Earthworm Book, How to Raise and Use Earthworms for Your Farm and Garden,* Emmaus: Rodale Press, 1977, p. 68.

16. W. G. Polack, *The Handbook to the Lutheran Hymnal,* Milwaukee: Northwestern Publishing House, 1975, p. 121.
17. C. A. Edwards and J. R. Lofty, *Biology of Earthworms,* Ontario, California: Bookworm Publishing, 1972.
18. Vol. 158, number 2, August, 1980, pp. 273-284.
19. Henry Morris, "The Influence of Evolution", in *The Twilight of Evolution*, Grand Rapids: Baker Book House, 1963, pp. 13-28.
20. Charles Darwin, *The Formation of Vegetable Mould,* Ontario, California: Bookworm Publishing Company, 1976, p. 148.

4.

CHARISMATICS ARE LIBERALS

One can claim a direct relationship between Luther's Reformation and the charismatic movement. The Reformed, first under the influence of Huldreich Zwingli (1484-1531) and later John Calvin (1509-1564), broke with Luther on the sacraments of Baptism and Holy Communion. Zwingli and Calvin taught that sacraments were only symbols, ordinances to be obeyed by man, not involving the work of God. The Church of England continued this doctrine, which John Wesley (1703-1791) adopted. Wesley's efforts resulted in the birth of Methodism, often called "the American religion" because of its growth and influence in the United States.

At the end of the 19th century, the followers of Wesley who thought the Methodists were becoming too liberal formed their own denominations, known for their emphasis on holiness or perfectionism. From these Wesleyan Holiness churches came the first Pentecostals. The best known today is the Assemblies of God, formerly the home of Rev. Jim Bakker and Rev. Jimmie Swaggart.

Charismatics are mainline members who have adopted the chief doctrine of the Pentecostals, tongues-speaking, while remaining in their liberal denominations. Pat Robertson, the founder of the Christian Broadcasting Network, is a charismatic Southern Baptist. Although the Pentecostals and charismatics make up two distinct groups within the American religious scene, charismatics continue to see such Pentecostal leaders as Oral Roberts as their spokesmen.

The American religious scene has long labored under the myth that charismatics are conservatives. One reason may be that some of them have publicly identified with conservative political causes. This should not be confused with a conservative or strict approach to the Scriptures. Many charismatics reject the inerrancy of Scripture and use the historical-critical method to justify their compromise. The characteristics of liberal theology match almost exactly the dominant themes of charismatics and Pentecostals. These parallels will be explored in the main body of this chapter.

Some may take offense at this chapter, since they think they left liberalism behind when they joined the tongues-speakers. A number of faithful, orthodox Lutheran pastors were once involved with the charismatic movement, before discovering the true nature of scriptural Christianity. At some point, someone knocked them on the head and said, "You are full of beans if you think the charismatic movement is the answer to the crisis in American Christianity." These Lutherans probably growled and fumed before they realized that they mistook froth for reality.

Today there are many charismatic ministers in the two largest Lutheran bodies in America, the Evangelical Lutheran Church in America and the Lutheran Church Missouri Synod. Several para-church groups exist to support the work of charismatic congregations within the mainline denominations. People are being deceived and seduced by the charismatics, who traverse the whole world to net a single convert and may only make him twice more fit for hell (Matthew 23:15). Some view the growth of Pentecostalism and the charismatic movement as signs of God's blessing A more realistic view is that the apostasy of the mainline denominations has become so obvious to members that they are driven from their congregations to those organizations which offer an alternative. Mainline ministers, too, have found comfort and support in their charismatic affiliations. The mainline churches teach against the Bible, while the Pentecostals and charismatics seem to view the Scriptures as authoritative.

The National Council of Churches could slow the growth of this phenomenon simply by going out of business. Of course, more is involved than just the crafts and assaults of the NCC. The entire mainline seminary system produces ministers who cannot preach the gospel because their faith has been undermined by the historical-critical method and a new religion of social and political activism has been substituted for the gospel. The Roman Catholic Church has joined this self-destructive crusade and found ways to outdo the liberal Protestants. Results:

1. Some Assemblies of God churches report half of their members to be former Catholics. A large proportion are former Lutherans.
2. Many mainline charismatics stay in their home congregations while floating over to the Assemblies of God for "spiritual enrichment."

Charismatics have properly diagnosed the ills of corpse-cold liberalism: lifeless worship, political harangues disguised as sermons, unbelieving ministers and officials, attacks on the Bible in the name of scholarship, and a lack of genuine Christian nurture. Unfortunately, their prescription for the ills of the church is killing the patient, slowly and painfully, just as liberalism did, while stimulating him to the appearance of life before his last gasp.

The fatal weakness of Pentecostalism and the charismatic movement is a trust in the operation of the Holy Spirit apart from the means of grace—their heritage of Reformed teaching. For them, God can and does speak directly to individuals, giving authoritative pronouncements on every possible subject. The dream they had last night is as authoritative as the Gospel of John, perhaps more so, since these visions can overturn the clear statements of Scripture. This is contrary to Scripture and the Lutheran Confessions, which declare that God comes to us only through the means of grace. Anything else is of the devil. Luther made this very clear in the Smalcald Articles:

> All this is the old devil and old serpent, who also converted Adam and Eve into enthusiasts, and led them from the outward Word of God to spiritualizing and self-conceit, and nevertheless he accomplished this through other outward words. Just as also our enthusiasts [at the present day] condemn the outward Word, and nevertheless they themselves are not silent, but they fill the world with their pratings and writings, as though, indeed, the Spirit could not come through the writings and spoken word of the apostles, but [first] through their writings and words He must come.[1]

A LITTLE HISTORY

Revivalism

The Pentecostal movement is old rather than new. Montanus (ca. 170), an early Christian heretic and current charismatic idol, said, "We will only take communion from Spirit-filled bishops." He and his two female assistants, who deserted their husbands to join Montanus, had many visions, including one of Christ in the

83

form of a female.[2]

The Wesleyan revivals of the early 19th century were Pentecostal in nature, with people fainting and dancing and jerking their limbs around. Then too, much of the work was in reclaiming inactive Christians who had fallen away from the church. The Wesleys were outcasts in the Episcopalian Church in England, shunned and persecuted by the approved clergy for being too earnest about scriptural principles, so the preaching was often done in open fields to the lower classes.

As Methodism (as it was called) became more respectable and academic, liberalism drove away elements loyal to the Wesleyan spirit, making Methodism even more liberal. Since the trend in all mainline churches was toward liberalism, from 1900 on, the growth of Pentecostalism owes some debt of gratitude to liberals for making the choice so obvious for people.

The Lutherans of the General Synod (now part of the Evangelical Lutheran Church in America) were also caught up with revivalism, which they felt would make the gospel more appealing. William Passavant (1821-1894), later a leader in the more conservative General Council, was a dedicated follower of the movement in his first pastorate. He studied Wesley instead of Luther and held "protracted meetings" until after midnight, where emotional excesses were common:

> Among the mourners or seekers and exhorters there was a confused mingling of tears, groans, cries and occasional loud shoutings. Praying, singing and exhorting often went on at the same time. The journal [of Passavant] records cases of persons falling to the floor and becoming as stiff as if dead.[3]

Lutheran advocates of the New Measures were so enchanted with Reformed doctrine that they proposed a new version of the Augsburg Confession in 1855 which omitted the doctrines offensive to the non-Lutheran Protestants—baptismal regeneration and the real presence of the body and blood of Christ in Holy Communion. The historic liturgy was also neglected by revivalistic Lutherans during this first era of marketing the gospel.

Pentecostalism

Revivalism took a new turn at Stone's Folly, a weird old house in Topeka, Kansas, where students of Charles F. Parham (a Wesleyan Holiness preacher) began speaking in tongues in 1901. They had decided, at his roughshod Bible institute, that the true mark of the Christian was baptism in the Holy Spirit, and that proof of this baptism was the ability to speak in tongues. Their study of the Acts of the Apostles, urged by Parham, had convinced them that true Christians are filled with the Holy Spirit and that proof of the Spirit is in glossolalia, or tongues-speaking. (All Pentecostal and charismatic theology hinges on this narrow understanding of Scripture.) The students' first efforts to speak in tongues did not pan out until they discovered the requirement to pray for the gift. After much struggle, the group obtained the desired proof. Some suspect that Parham already spoke in tongues and used this Bible study to manipulate his students into adopting his new style.

Pentecostalism flared up in earnest at the Azusa Street Mission in Los Angeles in 1906, with wildly emotional services, under the leadership of black preacher William J. Seymour, a student of Parham. Things got too wild for Seymour, so he had Parham come to Azusa Street to exert a calming influence. The two had a falling out and parted company.

The Pentecostals and charismatics owe much to Wesley, who described his Christian faith as a growth in stages. He was a humdrum and timid Christian until his experience at Aldersgate Church, where he felt his heart strangely warmed at hearing Luther's preface to Romans read. Lutherans would not call this a conversion or born-again experience, but illumination, an experience of deeper understanding or new insight.[4]

Wesley helped establish the notion that one could be a churchgoer all his life and not really be a Christian until this born-again experience happened. Many Lutheran missionaries, like Lars P. Esbjorn of the Augustana Synod, had a commitment to accept only "born-again" Christians to Holy Communion. This two-stage description of the Christian life made a perfect foundation for the claims of Pentecostals and charismatics, who often talk about being mere churchgoers until their baptism in the Holy Spirit.

Charismatic Renewal

Charismatic renewal, which is really Pentecostalism in the mainline groups, began in the Episcopal Church in California, when John and Joan Baker considered themselves baptized by the Holy Spirit in 1959, through the help of Pentecostal friends. This corrupt notion of a separate baptism will be considered later, but it is worth noting that charismatic flare-ups have been strongest in the most liberal denominations, those which had long abandoned the authority of Scripture. In many cases, the clergy trained in destructive criticism of the Bible, the historical-critical method, find joy and meaning in their ministry for the first time in decades through Pentecostalism. No one should be surprised that a minister or layman feels exhilarated after hearing that the miracles really happened, that Jesus is the Son of God, that prayer is something more than relaxation therapy.

After John and Joan Baker began speaking in tongues, they started working on friends and clergy. Dennis Bennett, an Episcopalian priest in a neighboring parish in Van Nuys, was drawn into the new phenomenon and found himself fired. Taking a poor parish in Seattle, he succeeded in spreading the practice even more, experiencing considerable church growth.[5]

Larry Christenson, an American Lutheran Church pastor in California, was distressed already in seminary with the demythologizing methods of the infidel Rudolph Bultmann. A member of the Foursquare Gospel Church in San Pedro, California, invited Christenson to a revival where a woman preached about the gifts of the Spirit. Later that night he began tongues-speaking and started influencing others. This happened about 1963. Christenson has remained a leader among Lutheran charismatics.[6] His opposition to the inerrancy of Scripture was echoed by other Lutheran charismatic leaders during the formation of the Evangelical Lutheran Church in America and gave great comfort to opponents of inerrancy. Christenson wrote in *Welcome Holy Spirit:*

> Charismatics would insist on the classic understanding and use of the historical-critical method of biblical interpretation, that is, the attempt to interpret Scripture according to the way it was meant by those who wrote it, and the way it was understood by those to whom it was addressed. . . .[7]

Erwin Prange was educated in the Missouri Synod, graduating in 1954 from Concordia, St. Louis, before serving in St. Louis County and later in New York City. Like Christenson, he had found little spiritual nurture in seminary. On December 7, 1963, after being involved with a Lutheran charismatic group and after requesting prayer for the ability to speak in tongues, he began tongues-speaking. Prange attended a pastoral conference where Harald Bredesen, the pastor of First Reformed in Mt. Vernon, New York, spoke about his charismatic experience. Prange also gave his testimony. Rev. Richard Neuhaus, in the Missouri Synod at that time, then with the ELCA, and now a Roman Catholic priest, spoke up and said:

> We can't walk away from this. These men have just made some of the most amazing statements ever heard in a Lutheran pastoral conference. Either they are liars, or they are crazy, or they are right. Either this is of God or of Satan. I don't think we can leave until we find out.[8]

The district president later warned Prange to keep this business quiet. When Prange spoke at the Lutheran Women's Missionary League meeting, he gave his charismatic testimony, to the chagrin of the district president. The husband of one of the women in attendance later "started a charismatic cell at [Concordia Seminary] Springfield that now numbers [in 1973] about thirty-five students."[9] Recently, Missouri Synod pastors have started Renewal In Missouri, a charismatic caucus within the LCMS.

Roman Catholic charismatics trace their origin to a 1966 group at Duquesne University, a Catholic institution. From there it spread to Notre Dame and Ann Arbor. Charismatic communes were established in South Bend, Indiana (where Notre Dame is located), and Ann Arbor, Michigan.

Tongues-speaking reached Yale through the Intervarsity Christian Fellowship in 1962, after two visits by Harald Bredesen (see the Prange experience above). The Ivy League enthusiasts were called "glosso-Yalies."[10] Tongues-speaking spread to Princeton and other academic centers where the Christian faith had been served up as thin, cold gruel. Mainline groups fought against charismatic ministers and congregations but finally accepted them in principle without taking them to heart. It may seem odd that two types of liberalism are at war with each other, but the main reason is their degree of liberalism. A truly dedicated liberal rejects most of the Bible, while a charismatic simply ignores significant sections.

Many institutions funded by Pentecostals led to the spread of the charismatic movement. The Full Gospel Business Men's Fellowship spread the word. David Wilkerson's *The Cross and the Switchblade* achieved almost canonical status among charismatics in the 1960s. (It was made into a film with Pat Boone as the minister and CHIPS star Eric Estrada as the hoodlum, later earning the Golden Turkey award as one of the worst religious movies ever made.)

Retreats (such as Cursillo and Kairos) and prayer groups too numerous to mention were used to lure unsuspecting people into the charismatic experience, with the claim that it was real Christianity, a higher form of the faith, or the only genuine manifestation of the church. People were not introduced to tongues-speaking at first, but desensitized about charismatic songs, charismatic worship, and charismatic doctrine. Mainline Christians were too puzzled or naive to say, "Phooey!" When compared to Bultmann's demythologizing of Christmas and Easter, tongues-speaking looked pretty good, for the minister as well as the layman.

DOCTRINAL ERRORS OF THE CHARISMATICS

Although the liberal tendencies of the tongues-speakers have already been mentioned, certain fundamental errors need to be discussed. When all of these matters have been carefully examined on the basis of the Scriptures, no one can claim that Pentecostalism is a conservative form of the Christian faith. Instead, tongues-speaking is an ecstatic religion which has attached itself, leechlike, to Christianity by selectively adopting its terminology.

Confusion about the Two Natures in Christ

Historic Christianity has always been the object of attack from false teachers, often concerning the two natures, human and divine, of Christ.[11] Liberals, laboring in the guise of Christians, cannot accept the divine nature of Christ: his pre-existence, his virgin birth, his miracles, his atoning death, and his resurrection. Pentecostals, in a similar fashion, assert that Jesus' "baptism" in the Holy Spirit enabled him to perform miracles.

Some corrections need to be noted at once. First of all, the Bible reveals Jesus' baptism in the Jordan as water baptism, with the Spirit descending upon him. There is no "baptism of the Holy Spirit" as a separate manifestation in the New Testament. Secondly, Jesus did not launch into a signs-and-wonders tongues-speaking ministry immediately afterwards but rejected Satan's pleas for such in his temptation in the desert. One despairs of finding any place in the Bible where Jesus spoke in tongues. More importantly, his divine nature was not installed when the Spirit descended, *contra* this notion:

> Jesus Christ was conceived of the Holy Ghost. . . . Why then must He be anointed? Because His human nature needed to be empowered by the Spirit, before even He could do successful service in this world. Jesus waited for thirty years until He was anointed. . .never forget that our Lord's ministry was not in the power of the second person of the blessed Trinity. . .but. . .the third.[12]

Pentecostals and charismatics draw this parallel— that we, like Jesus, can do nothing miraculous until baptized by the Holy Spirit. Until we experience that baptism, which is proven by tongues-speaking, we are not complete Christians. This concept of "anointing" by the Holy Spirit has also led to the charismatic tendency to call every book, video tape, TV program, and choir anthem "very anointed."

Pentecostals have displayed an unfortunate tendency to draw false and misleading parallels between themselves and Christ, claiming the authority of the Bible but showing no respect for the complete witness of Scripture.

Two Baptisms

Wesley's unfortunate misunderstanding about the Christian life led him to set the stage for his followers to teach two baptisms, water and Spirit. Much of Wesley's terminology was taken over by the Pentecostals, since he taught there was something beyond justification by faith, a deeper experience, which he called entire sanctification. Since he taught a waiting and a wrestling for this higher, deeper experience, Pentecostals converted the same into tarrying, yielding, and struggling for the "gift of tongues."

The distortions of Scripture are bad enough, but no one can calculate the damage these egregious errors cause to the spiritual well-being of believers. Although they deny it at first, Pentecostals believe they are the only true Christians. They cast doubt on genuine scriptural doctrine and steal from people the assurance of their salvation.

Since the Bible is the unified, unique revelation of God's will, no passage of Scripture contradicts another. Those who find contradictions realize later that the problems were induced by translators or a misunderstanding of the text. Thus, when Ephesians 4:5 states clearly that there is one baptism, we should not be able to find two baptisms anywhere else in Scripture. Pentecostals and charismatics find a second baptism precisely because they deny baptismal regeneration and need a validating substitute.

The move away from the sacraments of Baptism and Holy Communion, started by Zwingli and continued by Calvin during the Reformation, took away from people this visible reality of God's word. Since both men taught that the sacraments were only symbolic, man's witness to his faith, they undermined the certainty of salvation and created a craving for outward, visible proof. Thus, Pentecostals deny that Baptism and Holy Communion are sacraments while insisting upon tongues-speaking. Many seem angry that infants would be baptized, though entire households were baptized in Acts.

Pentecostals do not merely reject the sacraments; they are filled with wrath at the mention of them. The author was invited several years ago to a discussion of infant baptism, precipitated by an Assembly of God member who had raged against it. Since the group was mixed, the position of believer's baptism (opposed to infant baptism) was presented fairly, followed by an explanation of why the Scriptures clearly supported infant baptism. Though some claim that infants cannot believe, Psalm 22:9 speaks of a nursing infant believing, and Jesus said the kingdom of God belongs to little children (Mark 10:14). Though some argue that a baby cannot have faith, Christ himself taught that whoever did not receive the kingdom as a child would not receive it at all (Mark 10:15). During the entire discussion, the Assembly of God member folded her arms (a well-known body language expression of rejection) and glared.

Paul Crouch, Pentecostal owner of Trinity Broadcasting Network, offered "communion" on TV. He suggested that people get juice and crackers and follow along with him during the consecration, more properly the desecration. He picked up the bread, saying, "And Jesus said, ha-ha-ha, this is my body." (Crouch was indulging in what Pentecostals call holy laughter, another form of ecstatic speech.) On the same show they dedicated a baby named Destiny, Rev. Oral Roberts officiating. Oral pointed out that they did not believe in baptismal regeneration, in case any listener suspected them of Pentecostal unorthodoxy.

For charismatics and Pentecostals, tongues-speaking is the sacrament. At Jim Bakker's PTL Heritage Water Slide, people were known for stopping in the middle of the street for impromptu tongues-speaking sessions. Tongues-speaking is simply the repetition of meaningless sounds or syllables. In every case tongues-speaking is a learned behavior preceded by instruction and peer pressure to "come up higher and be with us." It has never been proven to be a foreign language. Like laughing and crying, it is easier to do in a group than alone, especially at first.

Jesus spoke of one baptism, water and Spirit, in John 3:5, in the discussion with Nicodemus. The Greek text could not be clearer, since water and Spirit are linked without the article, making it impossible to put asunder what God has joined together. "Most assuredly, I say to you, unless one is born of water and the Spirit, he cannot enter the kingdom of God" (RSV).

Pentecostals find separate baptisms in the Book of Acts. Acts 8:4-24 is a favorite passage to prove that a Spirit baptism can arrive later than water baptism. The intent of the two-baptism fallacy is to support the contention that one can be a baptized church member without really being a Christian. What Acts 8:15,16 states, according to R. C. H. Lenski, is that the Samaritans had received the supreme gifts of the Holy Spirit at their baptism, but the miraculous gifts of Pentecost later through the apostles.[13] The laying on of hands conferred the charismata of the Spirit, something Simon Magus wanted to buy, but the text does not tell us that the Samaritans spoke in tongues nor that they were "baptized by the Holy Spirit."

Pentecostals teach that the Holy Spirit is a reward bestowed by God upon those who earn it, through sacrifice, yielding, tarrying, and praying. That is the rabbinical understanding of the Holy Spirit, not the teaching of the Bible, which tells us that the Spirit is received as a gift through the sacrament of baptism.[14] Teaching tongues-speaking as a reward from God only serves to widen the gulf between Pentecostals and historic Christianity.

In Acts 10, Luke gave a lengthy account of the conversion of Cornelius and other Gentiles. The Holy Spirit fell on them during Peter's sermon. Jewish believers heard the Gentiles speak in tongues. Since God had bestowed the miracle of Pentecost upon the Gentiles, Peter exclaimed that they should be baptized. Here the work of the Spirit and baptism are too closely related to provide Pentecostals a foothold.

However, in Acts 19, Paul found some Ephesians who had been baptized into John's baptism but had not even heard of the Holy Spirit. Paul baptized them and laid hands on them. The Holy Spirit came upon them, and they spoke in tongues and prophesied (19:6). There is no way to make this into a two-baptism passage, since the only valid Christian baptism is in the name of Jesus or the Trinity. These people were not even aware of the Holy Spirit. One likely explanation is that the "disciples" were baptized earlier by a follower of John the Baptist. They failed the doctrinal test, since they had not been instructed. They failed the sacramental test, since they had not been baptized into Jesus but "into John."

Unscriptural Practices concerning Tongues

Nothing here is intended to imply that current tongues-speaking practices are the same as the day of Pentecost or anything genuine from the apostolic age. Paul's extensive discussion of tongues, 2 Corinthians 12-14, tell us much of what was going wrong in Corinth. Most forget that Corinth was a divided congregation and that the love chapter, 1 Corinthians 13, was aimed specifically at the charismatics. "If I speak with the tongues of angels and of men, but have not love. . . ." Paul hammered the tongue-speakers for their childishness. Some of the problems he noted among them were envy, showboating, pride, rudeness, selfishness, touchiness, evil thoughts, and rejoicing in iniquity. Tongues and prophecy, Paul warned, would all pass away.

Oral Roberts himself does not obey the injunction of Scripture to have one person speak in tongues and another prophesy. Tongue-speaking is the last gift listed in 1 Corinthians 12:28 and the only one requiring another gift. Oral teaches that one can speak in tongues and do one's own interpreting, getting a direct revelation from God without intermediaries, a revelation which actually suggests that the Bible is insufficient and unclear. Oral rejects baptismal regeneration. On one television show, Oral and his son Richard climbed into a swimming pool in their business suits and poured water on each other. Wouldn't it be better to believe God's word than to mock baptism? ". . .according to his mercy he saved us, through the washing of regeneration and renewing of the Holy Spirit" (Titus 3:5).

Interpreting tongues is a serious problem for charismatics. First of all, despite all anecdotal claims, no contemporary Pentecostal has ever shown a magical ability to speak in a foreign language without studying the language first. The tongues-speaking stories are so similar that they take on a liturgical form. The following is the tongues-speaking anecdote which the author has heard or read in many different versions:

> I was speaking in [name of foreign country]. Someone came up to me and said, "Where did you learn to speak perfect [name of foreign language]?" I replied, "Why, I have never spoken a word of [name of language] in my life!" Then the stranger said to me, "I have a master's degree in [name of language] and I can tell you that your speech was perfect in grammar and pronunciation."[15]

Some of us have heard or read the same claim in

many forms, with such languages as ecclesiastical Latin and Japanese in the appropriate blanks. Enthusiasts smile smugly while the story is being told, without names, dates, places, with less evidence than a judge would demand for a parking ticket. Despite the hundreds of examples of flawless and instantaneous speeches in another language, charismatic and Pentecostal schools continue to pay people to teach foreign languages to their tongues-speaking students.

In fact, modern tongue-speaking is nothing more than ecstatic speech, easy to learn with peer pressure and some experience. Many people fall into it and fall out of it in a period of time. Each one has his own style, though there is a lot of imitation. One woman said, "Sh-sh-sh-sh-ba-ba-ba-ta-ta-ta." Others affect a biblical "Shonda kabul togandaatol." The same nonsense can be heard at football games:"Bulldogs, bulldogs, bow-wow-wow. Eli Yale." An honest charismatic said he kept up tongues-speaking because of his childish addiction to emotionalism. Many of his friends, he said, acted like they opened a plug and let their brains run out.

How can one interpret gibberish? One can listen to "interpretation" on the record included in *The Charismatic Movement,* edited by Michael Hamilton.[16] After some "Na-ga-ka-bom" a woman spoke up (in defiance of 1 Corinthians 14:34) and said, "Listen to what the Spirit of God says. Don't be shallow in reading the Scriptures. Look deeply into them." If the Holy Spirit chose to speak to that congregation, surely he would have said something a little more profound. At one Pentecostal service a woman stood up and said, "The Holy Spirit has led me into a lot of congregations and out of a lot of congregations. Here they really teach the word of God." This seems to be a case of the Holy Spirit being used to validate a woman's feelings.

Women in Leadership Roles

Women pastors are absolutely forbidden in Scriptures (1 Timothy 2:12), an undebatable *datum* until Pentecostalism and liberalism converged in the charismatic movement. The Pentecostals beat the liberals in establishing female ministers in their churches. The mainline churches barely got started with the ordination of women ministers after World War II, some waiting until 1970. The Pentecostals were active much earlier. Even in mainline churches, women normally did not even seek to lead in worship until the ferment of the 1960s worked its way through the churches. Now there are several TV Pentecostal ministers who let their wives preach for them. One allowed that she was dedicated to being "brassy for the Lord." In fact, no woman minister can be legitimately called a pastor, for her claim to ordination is at war with the word of God.

God intended that men would be leaders in the church, not to oppress and suppress women, but to let men develop their normally stunted spiritual lives. Women in liberal denominations often confess that they do not want a woman minister and that they prefer having their husbands take leadership roles. They have seen the male leadership of their congregations evaporate in the face of feminist demands. In traditional Christian denominations, like the Wisconsin Synod and the Evangelical Lutheran Synod, women have more influence (in the proper sense) rather than less. Everyone wins. In liberal groups and Pentecostal/charismatic gatherings, aggressive women gain at the expense of those who learn quietly, the majority of women. Everyone loses.

Theology of the Cross

Charismatic and Pentecostal ministers have sought to validate their teaching by the display of "signs and wonders," and by their success stories, measured in terms of money and members. Until the disasters which befell certain television ministers, they seemed to be unusually blessed, and they never seemed to tire of letting people know how successful they were.

The only criterion for measuring the success of a pastor, according to Luther, is whether he teaches pure doctrine according to Scripture.[17] Therefore, the faithful Christian should expect the cross, not glory. Luther explains:

> Secondly, God permits His saints to suffer these trials as an example for others, both to alarm the carnally secure and to comfort the timid and alarmed. . . . But when we see and hear that God has in like manner dealt with His saints and did not spare even His own mother, we have the knowledge and comfort that we need not despair in our trials, but remain quiet and wait until He helps us, even as He has helped all His saints.[18]

But, some would counter, does not God bless those churches which are faithful to his word? Rather than seek an easy equation, which would give anti-Christian cults the greatest honor for the fastest church growth, we should listen to Luther, who saw great calamities and poverty come with the Reformation:

> Not only is Christ hidden from the world, but a still harder thing is it that in such trials Christ conceals himself even from His church, and acts as if He had forgotten, aye, had entirely forsaken and rejected it, since He permits it to be oppressed under the cross and subjected to all the cruelty of the world, while its enemies boast, glory and rejoice over it, as we shall hear in the next Gospel.[19]

Thus we should be very careful not to imitate the doctrinal errors of the charismatics.

CHARACTERISTICS SHARED BY LIBERALS AND CHARISMATICS

Subjectivity

The founder of modern theology was Friedrich Schleiermacher (the last name means "one who makes a veil, screen or haze"), who established in the early 19th century that one could be an accepted theologian without believing in the basic doctrines of the faith. In this sense he is truly the founder of modern theology. He has exerted a considerable influence on such modern theologians as Karl Barth and Paul Tillich. Schleiermacher defined the Christian faith as "a feeling of absolute dependence." From his time forward it has been acceptable to talk about Christianity subjectively, as a feeling rather than a certainty derived from God's objective word. C. F. W. Walther understood the danger of subjectivity:

> But the required feeling may rest on a false foundation. It may not be the testimony of the Holy Spirit in the heart, but a physical effect, produced by the lively presentations of the preacher. That explains why sincere persons who have become believers not infrequently feel one moment that they have found the Lord Jesus, and in the next, that they have lost Him again. [20]

Schleiermacher paved the way for using theological terms while changing their meanings. Charismatics and Pentecostals use the same approach today, deluding many uninformed people. Proof can be found in the number of people who justify what they believe or where they worship by how they feel.

Schleiermacher and the growth of rationalism

opened the way for Pentecostals and charismatics to offer themselves as a positive alternative to liberalism. However, the tongues-speaking movement is itself a liberal phenomenon and only makes matters worse by appearing to be a conservative approach to the Bible. Liberalism is the rejection of any biblical doctrine, not just rejection of certain modern elements, such as the rationalistic interpretation of miracles. Whenever the Bible is used selectively, serious errors will follow in time, even if the initial problems seem slight and harmless.

Luther was not against reason, but he distinguished between the magisterial and the ministerial use of reason.[21] The liberals know only the magisterial use of reason, judging which Scripture passages they consider true or authoritative. (*Magister* is Latin for master.) When a charismatic was reminded of Paul's injunction against false teachers, Romans 16:17,18, she quickly replied, "That's why I prefer Jesus to Paul." As if Jesus tolerated false doctrine! Our Lord said, "Anyone who breaks one of the least of these commandments and teaches others to do the same will be called least in the kingdom of heaven, but whoever practices and teaches these commands will be called great in the kingdom of heaven" (Matthew 5:19 NIV) .

One example of the ministerial use of reason is studying the geography of the Holy Land to help in understanding the content of God's word. Anyone who wants to know the actual content of the word of God is employing the ministerial use of reason. (*Minister* means servant in Latin.) Luther opposed placing human reason or feelings above the word of God:

> To this I reply: I have often said before that feeling and faith are two different things. It is the nature of faith not to feel, to lay aside reason and close the eyes, to submit absolutely to the Word, and to follow it in life and

death.[22]

Ecumenism, Unionism by Another Name

Tongues-speaking spread in liberal Protestant bodies because the members were sacrament-starved. Thomas Merton, the Trappist monk who grew up a liberal Protestant, wrote in *The Seven Storey Mountain* about the arid intellectuals who served as liberal Protestant ministers. One minister could speak glibly about the novels of D. H. Lawrence, but could not talk about Christ.

As mainline members, Protestant and Catholic, became distressed over the clergy's assault on the Bible and support of political activism, they found a common solution in this new movement. The new sacrament of tongues-speaking created by Pentecostals has united all church bodies, many of them already used to ecumenical services, whether sponsored by liberal groups associated with the National Council of Churches or more conservative leaders like Billy Graham. The confession of faith is usually not, "I am a Catholic (or Lutheran or Baptist) charismatic," but "I am a charismatic." There is instant identification and fellowship among all charismatics and Pentecostals, with certain key words used to signal a common identity: Spirit-filled, on fire, praise, prayer group, and healing service. If charismatics were genuinely conservative, they would have qualms about the varying doctrinal standards of other groups. However, the common saying among charismatics is: "Doctrine divides." Indeed. Doctrine divides the sheep from the goats.

While unionism has been popular in recent years, the church leaders of the past understood how joint worship without doctrinal agreement led to or sprang from doctrinal laxity. Martin Reu observed:

> Doctrinal indifference is at once the root of unionism and its fruit. Whoever accepts, in theory as well as in practice, the absolute authority

of the Scriptures and their unambiguousness with reference to all fundamental doctrines, must be opposed to every form of unionism.[23]

New Revelations Transmitted through the Emotions

When the liberals tried to take away the Scriptures as the ruling norm for Christians, they had to find a substitute. Denatured Christianity went one of two ways, toward rationalism and ultimately Unitarianism, or toward emotionalism, ultimately Pentecostalism. They also needed new revelations to replace the true revelation of God, his word. For the rationalists, the new religion, which they called the religion of Jesus, was social activism. For the emotionalists, the new religion was tongues-speaking.

Charismatics have a flexible view of the Bible. The ruling norm for them is the latest vision experienced by one of their leaders. Someone announces, "I had a word of knowledge. We should send Jim as a missionary to Bulgaria." If everyone agrees, it is judged a word of knowledge. If the revelation is a dud, someone has a new insight. An observer described Pentecostals as operating like a school of fish, swimming in one direction and then suddenly moving as one in a new direction, for no apparent reason. The heart of the issue, however, is that the "word of knowledge" displaces the Bible as the ruling norm. This implies that the Scriptures are incomplete, insufficient, and unclear.

After being clobbered in debates when trying to argue from Scripture, the Council of Trent used this line of argument against the Lutherans:

> The method of debate on the part of the papalists is far different now than it was at the time of Eck, Emser, and others like them. These men did not refuse to fight with us with the weapons of the Scripture. Pighius, however, has

perceived that this arrangement has done the papal kingdom more harm than good. Therefore he has shown a different and shorter way by which, provided they stuck to it, they could obtain practically anything without trouble. It consists in this that they bring together every oratorical device and then declaim loudly about the shortness, the incompleteness, the insufficiency, ambiguity, and obscurity of the Scripture and strenuously fight for the necessity, authority, perfection, certainty, and clarity of the unwritten traditions.[24]

If we could publish a list of every revelation of God claimed by all the charismatics and Pentecostals, the world would groan from the weight. Besides implicitly denying the inspiration and authority of Scriptures, these special revelations manipulate people and place a terrible burden on the gullible, as many insiders have admitted. In fact, too many direct communications from the Holy Spirit sound like the vindictive side of the person speaking. Charismatics are quick to say that their critics are possessed by Satan, but the hallmarks of Pentecostal worship are well established in the worship of Satan: being "slain in the Spirit," phoney tongue-speaking, ecstatic dancing and laughter, miraculous signs, and trances. Genuine tongues-speaking is in the Bible, but its abuse is subjected to considerable criticism in 1 Corinthians 12-14. If the charismatics are keen about the Bible, they should memorize this particular passage, spoken by Jesus:

Not everyone who says to me, "Lord, Lord" will enter the kingdom of heaven, but only he who does the will of my Father who is in heaven. Many will say to me on that day, "Lord, Lord, did we not prophesy in your name, and *in your name drive out demons and perform many miracles*?" Then I will tell them plainly, "I never knew you. Away from me, you evildoers!" (Matthew 7:21-23)

Ordination of Women

If anything shows doctrinal agreement between liberals, charismatics, and Pentecostals, it is the ordination of women. 1 Timothy 3:2 is clear enough, saying the minister is to be the husband of one wife. Paul also said clearly that he did not allow a woman to be in authority over a man in spiritual matters (1 Timothy 2:12). A Pentecostal woman minister argued that the Timothy passage did not mean what it seemed to say. She said, "We don't take the words, 'This is my body, literally, so why should we take 1 Timothy 2:12 literally?" Recently, a Pentecostal minister said on TV, "Isn't it great that we ordain women now?"

One woman minister, a former bartender, spoke on TV about her change of vocation. She wanted to speak in tongues, so she put candles on each corner of her bathtub and baptized herself, repeatedly saying, "Yabba-dabba-doo." Her atavistic cry (from the cartoon show, "The Flintstones") got her warmed up for speaking in tongues. The interviewer and audience laughed heartily at this sacrilege.

She was simply continuing a long line of self-appointed women ministers and cult leaders: Aimee Semple McPherson (adulteress and founder of the Four Square Gospel Church); Katharine Kuhlman (homewrecker, Pentecostal, an early media star); Mary Baker Eddy (founder of the Christian Scientists); and Ellen G. White, (plagiarist and founder of the Seventh Day Adventists). If another woman tried to outdo White, she simply fell over in a trance and popped up with a more glamorous vision. The potency of local charismatic cells within mainline churches comes largely from the leadership of women.

Ill-educated Clergy: Rote Memory of Dogma,

Shallow Dogmatism

Liberalism thrives on ignorance of the word. When the clergy know Hebrew and Greek, studying the Scriptures in humility, false doctrine is denied a healthy start, just as weeds have trouble growing in a healthy, well-fed lawn. Classical mainline Protestantism has made impressive gains in the formation of political activists by concentrating on theories about Scripture as opposed to the actual content of the Bible. Thus students of liberal seminaries graduate with little Latin and less Greek, but are imbued with a narrow and fierce dogmatism about the current fads. In fact, liberal seminary graduates do not even know the literature of their own denomination's past, because the professors scoff at it and seldom assign it. Take a tour of a mainline seminary bookstore and read the texts listed as required reading; then ask for the classical theological publications of the church body. One person asked for the books of a deceased seminary professor at one bookstore, at the school where the late professor taught for decades. The store manager said, "How do you spell his name?" Then she said, "Who publishes it?" Upstairs, a room in the library was named in honor of the man, R. C. H. Lenski.

Pentecostals graduate from the College of the Holy Spirit. One joke is that they attend a Bible college until the studying gets tough. Then God speaks, "Go to Fergus Falls and build me a church." Jim and Tammie Bakker left college after one year. Pentecostal denominations have light ordination requirements, and they also train people in a narrow dogmatism. A Pentecostal in Alaska will answer a doctrinal question exactly the same way as a tongues-speaker in Delaware.

In a similar fashion, charismatics are self-appointed ambassadors of the Holy Spirit. John Sherrill, the son of a theology professor at Union Theological School in New York City, wrote that he did not know, after ten years as an editor of *Guideposts*, if Jesus was the Son of God.[25] Influenced by the charismatic Catherine Marshall, he attended tongues-speaking services, went to charismatic prayer groups, and eventually spoke in tongues. In his book, *They Speak with Other Tongues,* 1970, he announced that he was no longer a disciple after learning tongues-speaking, but suddenly an "apostle." Imagine the fate of any ordained critic of this self-appointed apostle! It would be like arguing with God! (At least God listens.)

Rote memory of doctrine and narrow dogmatism are the results of shallow training. A current standard of liberal, feminist exegesis makes much of Jesus as a mother hen. Likewise, a canon of all Pentecostal exegesis states: "Jesus Christ, the same yesterday, today, and forever" (Hebrews 13:8). The verse is followed by tumultuous shouts at Pentecostal rallies, because they teach that Christ was unable to do miracles until he received the Holy Spirit. Therefore, they believe that they, like Christ, will do the same miracles because they possess the Holy Spirit. Liberal dogmatism is always changing, flitting from one destructive opiate to another. Charismatics have moved from mere tongues-speaking to occultic imaging and worse, always looking for the latest thrill. Mainline liberals and charismatics together are dabbling in the occult: spirit guides and imaging.

The Swaggart and Bakker cases serve to remind us that the Assemblies of God do not discipline ministers very well. One minister was so bad, in spite of his enormous success, that the Assemblies booted him out. His name? Paul Yonggi Cho. Cho revealed his depraved theology in *The Fourth Dimension*, 1979, found in many Christian bookstores today. In brief, Cho teaches that one must demand from God exactly what one wishes. This is occultic imaging, and it is found in various forms among the American televangelists. Some call it "faith" theology, since the results depend on one's faith rather than on God's powers. One example of demanding miracles is from Cho's own life, after he failed to receive the bike, desk, and chair he prayed for:

> Then that still small voice welled up in my soul, and the Spirit said, "My son, I heard your prayer a long time ago." Right away I blurted out, "Then where are my desk, chair, and bicycle?" The Spirit then said, "Yes, that is the trouble with you, and with all my children. They beg me, demanding every kind of request, but they ask in such vague terms that I can't answer. Don't you know that there are dozens of kinds of desks, chairs and bicycles? But you've simply asked me for a desk, chair and bicycle. You never ordered a specific desk, chair or bicycle." That was a turning point in my life. No professor in the Bible college ever taught me along these lines.[26]

A flattering introduction to *The Fourth Dimension* is provided by the noted mainline preacher, Robert Schuller (Reformed Church in America). Schuller declares, without blushing:

> Don't try to understand it. Just start to enjoy it! It's true. It works. I tried it. Thank you—Paul Yonggai Cho—for allowing the Holy Spirit to give this message to us and to the world. God loves you and so do I.[27]

The secular form of this teaching was first promoted by Napoleon Hill (1883-1970) in *Think and Grow Rich*, first published in 1937, still a continuing best-seller in the secular market, published by Ballantine Books, 1983.

Cho continues to be greatly admired by Pentecostals and charismatics. In 1990 Pat Robertson, the founder of Christian Broadcasting Network and CBN University, invited Rev. Paul Y. Cho to be on his Christian talk show, "The 700 Club," and played a promotional tape about the growing Cho empire: a 600,000-member church in Seoul, Korea; a newspaper; broadcasting; and his International Church Growth Institute, where hundreds of American and foreign pastors are trained by Cho, C. Peter Wagner (Fuller Seminary), and Rev. Jack Hayford (Foursquare Gospel Church).

Pat Robertson has also promoted occultic ideas in his book on *The Secret Kingdom.*[28] Robertson has deliberately tried to Christianize the message of Napoleon Hill:

> Unfortunately, such people as Napoleon Hill, who wrote *Think and Grow Rich,* have gleaned only a few of the truths of the kingdom of God. They try to gain the kingdom without submitting themselves to the King. Some of the metaphysical principles of the kingdom, taken by themselves, can produce fantastic temporal benefits. But without the lordship of Jesus, these benefits are both transitory and harmful. In fact, many of the advocates of mind over matter ultimately end in hellish spiritism (p. 69).

Despite Robertson's warnings, his own doctrine suffers from an awe of worldly success and power:

> Once we perceive this secret, we realize anew that the Bible is not an impractical book of theology, but rather a practical book of life containing a system of thought and conduct that will guarantee success (p. 44).

> We must hear this before it is too late: Jesus has opened to us the truths of the secret world of God! He has given us entrance into a world of indescribable power (p. 51).

Contrast Robertson, Schuller, and Cho with the biblical understanding of Luther: "If only the preachers remain orthodox and the doctrine is preserved, God will grant grace that among the multitude there will always be some who will accept the Word; for where the Word is pure and unadulterated, it cannot be without fruit."[29]

Needless to say, liberals looking for a thrill are thronging to the New Age Movement. They find no contradiction between taking Holy Communion and visiting a medium to speak with the dead. Like charismatics, they are looking for power but are not too careful about where it comes from. They are anxious to deny the occultic label.

Excommunication

More than one person has huffed that conservative denominations actually excommunicate people, an expression of doctrinal and moral discipline with considerable foundation in Scripture (Matthew 18). Liberals, charismatics, and Pentecostals all excommunicate with resolute firmness and single-minded purpose. To fall from grace, one only needs to question a single doctrine. For a liberal, it might be the doctrine of abortion on demand. For a charismatic, it might be the value of prayer groups. The method used is shunning, a freeze-out. This is how liberals and Pentecostals have extended their influence everywhere, by making it clear what happens to dissenters. Yes, liberals and charismatics will love-bomb someone who indicates a willingness to become a convert, but they disown even the mildest critics.

Liberals and charismatics confuse the innocent by denying the very labels they use of themselves. A Left-wing nun engaged in a rhetorical smokescreen about her support of the Sandinistas in Central America, ending in her declaration that Fidel Castro was not a Marxist. She then equated Marxist revolution with the Fourth of July. Likewise, in a conversation with a faith-healer: "Are you charismatic?" Answer: "No."

Several diagnostic questions followed. Then came the confession: "I'm Third Wave. We are no longer distinguishing ourselves from the Evangelicals. We are blending together." He was right. By failing to assert themselves, Evangelicals have seen their institutions taken over by charismatics. While Evangelical Protestants once firmly opposed Pentecostalism, now they refuse to identify false doctrine as such. Such blending is always a capitulation.

Work Righteousness

The article on which the church stands or falls is number four of the Augsburg Confession, justification by grace through faith, apart from the works of the law:

> Also they teach, that men cannot be justified before God by their own strength, merits, or works, but are freely justified for Christ's sake through faith, when they believe that they are received into favor and that their sins are forgiven for Christ's sake, who, by His death, hath made satisfaction for our sins. This faith God imputes for righteousness in his sight. (Romans 4: 3,4)

The liberal problem with this article, the foundation of Protestantism, is that liberals reject the atoning death of Christ. The standard, puerile line is worded thus: "There was no celestial equation made." John Dillenberger and Claude Welch, educated at Harvard and Yale, expressed themselves even more clearly: "This is his work of atonement (or 'at-one-ment'), not some external or 'magical' act whereby God is appeased and man made righteous." (The real work of atonement, according to Welch and Dillenberger, was the potency of his God-consciousness, which inspired men "to realize in their own lives that which Jesus embodied.")[30] Liberals can only make a moralistic, legalistic philosophy out of the Christian faith. They find salvation, therefore, in a crescendo of save-the-world campaigns, each one resulting in making matters worse for everyone, except people who run save-the-world campaigns.

The charismatic version of works-righteousness is displayed in the frantic need to prove the validity of the movement through miracles, numerical growth, and prosperity. Though all might justifiably pray that God's Kingdom grow, the emphasis upon outward proof rather than pure doctrine can only result in a man-centered, even a me-centered religion, as Paul Y. Cho has proved.

Political Power

The thirst for political power among liberals is established beyond a doubt. The mainline churches have established a huge network of lobbying organizations across North America. The National Council of Churches is the official headquarters, but the work done by the NCC is multiplied by denominational counterparts and interlocking activist groups. So-called denominational hunger funds mostly feed hungry lobbyists while deluding faithful members about sending food to Africa. Women's groups pursue pro-abortion policies, lobby for quotas, and take carefully managed tours to Marxist countries, coming home all a-flutter about the charm and wit of Fidel Castro. Edmund and Julia Robb have documented all this in *The Betrayal of the Church, Apostasy and Renewal in the Mainline Denominations.*[31] Carefully researched articles on the subject can be obtained from the Institute for Religion and Democracy, 729 15th Street NW, Suite 900, Washington, D.C. 20005.

Pentecostals have completed their "Washington for Jesus" 1988 campaign, a similar approach to power on the Potomac. One liberal lobbyist for a mainline denomination angrily declared that the overt religious emphasis was a mask for a covert political effort. His jowls shook with rage, even though he regularly bragged about using his clout as a church official to influence legislation. Nevertheless, he was correct. The Pentecostals and charismatics hunger for secular power in D.C. Pat Robertson and others have made some impressive inroads in politics simply by organizing the Pentecostals and charismatics who have not participated actively in the political process. The problem, as Jerry Falwell seems to have learned, is that when the church (or a minister) seeks to have power in the world, spiritual power is lost.

The next few years will confirm the postulate that charismatics and their elder brothers in the faith, the Pentecostals, are liberal in doctrine and rushing headlong toward complete apostasy. As their preaching of the law becomes more and more muted, to match the temper of the time, the tongues-speaking groups will accommodate themselves ever more obligingly to today's morals, fads, and delusions.

NOTES

1. Smalcald Articles, Part III, Article VIII, 5-6, *Concordia Triglotta*, St. Louis: Concordia Publishing House, 1921, p. 495. Pieper, *Christian Dogmatics*, III, p. 130.

2. Arthur J. Clement, *Pentecost or Pretense? An Examination of the Pentecostal and Charismatic Movements*, Milwaukee: Northwestern Publishing House, 1981, p. 19. Otto Heick, *A History of Christian Thought, 2 vols.*, Philadelphia: Fortress Press, 1965, I, p. 78. W. J. Hollenweger, *The Pentecostals, The Charismatic Movement in the Churches*, Minneapolis: Augsburg Publishing House, 1972.

3. G. H. Gerberding, *Life and Letters of W. A. Passavant,* Greenville: The Young Lutheran, 1906, p. 83.

4. Heinrich Schmid, *Doctrinal Theology of the Evangelical Lutheran Church*, Minneapolis: Augsburg Publishing House, no date, pp. 450-458. Schmid is a classic compilation of orthodox Lutheran dogmatics, invaluable for pastors and theologians.

5. Richard Quebedeux, *The New Charismatics, II*, New York: Harper and Row, 1983, pp. 61ff. The Full Gospel Business Men's Fellowship, organized in 1951 by Oral Roberts and Demos Shakarian, succeeded in mixing Pentecostalism with the mainlines.

6. Larry Christenson, *The Charismatic Renewal Among Lutherans*, Minneapolis: Lutheran Charismatic Renewal Services, 1976.

7. Minneapolis: Augsburg Publishing House, 1987, pp. 45-6, cited in Craig S. Stanford, *The Death of the Lutheran Reformation, A Practical Look at Modern Theology and Its Effects on the Church and in the Lives of its People,* Ft. Wayne: Stanford Publishing, 1988, p. 251.

8. Erwin Prange, *The Gift Is Already Yours,* Plainfield: Logos International, 1973, p. 57.

9. *Ibid.*, p. 77. Apparently this cell operated in 1973. The seminary has since moved to Ft. Wayne and become known for curing students of charismatic doctrine.

10. Quebedeaux, *op. cit.,* p. 129.

11. Martin Chemnitz, *The Two Natures in Christ,* translated by J. A. O. Preus, St. Louis: Concordia Publishing House, 1971.

12. F. B. Meyer, *A Castaway and Other Addresses,* Chicago: Revell, 1897, p. 86. Cited in Frederick Dale Bruner, *A Theology of the Holy Spirit* (Grand Rapids: Eerdmans, 1970), p. 221n. Bruner presents a devastating but fair portrayal of Pentecostal theology and biblical exegesis. Some may think the Meyer quote is dated, but

the same explanation, of Jesus' inability to perform miracles until "baptized by the Holy Spirit" was broadcast on religious TV, while this chapter was being written.

13. *Interpretation of the Acts of the Apostles*, Columbus, Ohio: Lutheran Book Concern, 1934, p. 319.

14. Bruner, *op. cit.*, pp. 173, 183.

15. This story was told about a Pentecostal in Japan. The exact same wording is used for a story about someone speaking perfect Hebrew in *The Pentecostals, the Charismatic Movement in the Churches*, by W. J. Hollenweger, Minneapolis: Augsburg Publishing House, 1972, p. 4.

16. Grand Rapids: W. B. Eerdmans, 1975.

17. C. F. W. Walther, *The Proper Distinction between Law and Gospel*, St. Louis: Concordia Publishing House, 1928, p. 423.

18. *Sermons of Martin Luther, 8 vols., II,* p. 40f.

19. *Sermons of Martin Luther, 8 vols., III,* p. 67, (John 10:11-16).

20. C. F. W. Walther, *op. cit., p.* 135.

21. Siegbert Becker, *The Foolishness of God*, Milwaukee: Northwestern Publishing House, 1982.

22. *Sermons of Martin Luther, 8 vols.* II, p. 244.

23. *In the Interest of Lutheran Unity, Two Lectures*, Columbus: The Lutheran Book Concern, 1940, p. 20.

24. Martin Chemnitz, *Examination of the Council of Trent*, 4 vols., translated by Fred Kramer, St. Louis: Concordia Publishing House, 1971, I, p. 71.

25. *They Spoke in Other Tongues.*

26. *The Fourth Dimension, The Key to Putting Your Faith to Work for a Successful Life*, South Plainfield: Bridge Publishing, 1979, p. 12.

27. *Ibid.*, unpaginated foreword.

28. Pat Robertson, *The Secret of the Kingdom.*

29. *What Luther Says. An Anthology,* 3 vols., ed. Ewald Plass, St. Louis: Concordia Publishing House, 1959, III, p. 1125.

30. *Protestant Christianity,* New York: Charles Scribner, 1958, p. 222.

31. Westchester, Illinois: Crossway Books, 1986.

5.

DEFENDING MORALITY

Anyone who tries to discuss contemporary moral issues finds himself enmeshed in well-rehearsed arguments which do not seem to address the real issues. For this reason, many orthodox Christians feel constrained to withdraw from the field of battle rather than endure the aggravation of reasoning against emotional tirades and visceral attacks.[1]

The debater must be able to identify and defuse the logical fallacies which are a staple of all bad arguments. Not only does this leave the opponent sputtering, but it also can impress an audience which otherwise would be victimized by personal attacks, emotional appeals and subtle deceptions.

Logical fallacies are as old as ancient Greece and Rome, where public debate formed policy. For this reason many fallacies are still identified with Latin terms. Lawyers and debaters learn these fallacies and their antidotes. Politicians revel in them. Shouldn't Christians study them as well? This chapter will illustrate some of the most common fallacies and defenses against them. One may obtain many more examples from circuit meetings, family discussions and TV editorials. Lewis Carroll wrote in *Alice in Wonderland:*

"In my youth," said his father, "I took to the law,
And argued each case with my wife;
And the muscular strength, which it gave to my jaw,
Has lasted the rest of my life."

Lewis Carroll also wrote *Symbolic Logic* in 1896.

MATERIAL FALLACIES OF RELEVANCE

These do not rely on ambiguous language, the wrong use of words, but on the distortion of facts.

The *ad hominem* (against the man)

The most popular fallacy continues to be the most useful. Weak arguments cannot be won by debating the issues. The *ad hominem* is used to deflect the argument away from the facts and toward the person. "Nazi" is a favorite term. If the believer tries to say, "I'm not a Nazi," then he has already fallen into the trap. A better approach would be to define the Nazi philosophy or to identify the characteristics of Nazi leaders. He could say, "You used the term Nazi about me, but is it really accurate? I have no sympathies with them."

Heirs of the spirit of compromise may respond to an orthodox Lutheran by calling him a "Fundamentalist." This infuriates some Lutherans, who know they are not Fundamentalists. However, some non-Lutherans consider the term a positive description of someone who believes scriptural doctrine. A balanced answer to the charge of Fundamentalism would be: "Fundamentalist? If you mean that I believe in the basic doctrines of the Bible, such as inerrancy, creation, the virgin birth, and the resurrection, then I would call myself a Fundamentalist. But if you are suggesting that I believe in the earthly reign of the Messiah, then I would have to disagree and ask you to use more precise terms. Like Luther, I am simply stating my trust in the Holy Scriptures, in all of the Bible, not just parts of it."

The final statement is an opportunity to confess the truth of the Bible. Then the issue is no longer whether the person is a Fundamentalist, but what Luther taught. An editor once wrote a letter which said, in effect, "Prove to me that the Wisconsin Synod is not a Fundamentalist group." He combined an *ad hominem* with an *ad ignorantiam* (discussed below).

Deflecting the *ad hominem* might be preferred to a frontal attack on the content of the fallacy. The deflection is simple: "I would rather stick to the issues." Taking the high road is always a better approach with a discerning audience.

People have piled up a host of terms for use when the battle is being lost, so that they can insist sanctimoniously: "You are being judgmental. You are a sexist. You are homophobic." The value of any particular term increases with public acceptance, which subsequently grows with use by the print and broadcast media. A response to the accusation of being judgmental, a term borrowed from psychologist Carl Rogers, might be: "Of course I use my judgment. I hope that doctors, lawyers, nurses, and teachers all use their judgment, to choose between good and evil, right and wrong. You may remember that Nixon claimed to have used bad judgment." Sexist? Why not ask whether feminism really benefits women. Homophobic? "I'm not afraid of men. That's what 'homophobic' means."

The victim of name-calling should consider the effort a great compliment and act accordingly. The intent of the *ad hominem* is to anger the opponent and seduce the audience. An angry response to an *ad hominem* fallacy creates in the audience the very impression of malice which the non-believer wants to prove. Name-calling is not new. Jesus told us, "Blessed are you when men revile you and persecute you and utter all kinds of evil against you falsely on my account. Rejoice and be glad, for your reward is great in heaven, for so men persecuted the prophets who were before you." (Matthew 5:11,12 RSV).

The *tu quoque* (and you too)

Small children catch on to this fallacy right away. If one child says, "You're a pig," the other responds, "You are too!" The *tu quoque* is simply a bad response to an *ad hominem*. When issues are being discussed, people often use the *tu quoque* with impunity. Hearing that someone is in favor of capital punishment but opposed to abortion, a person declares, "How can you claim to care about life when you openly support killing criminals?" In basic terms, the argument involves this exchange:

Pro-life - Abortion is murder and therefore unjust.
Pro-abortion - You are killing people unjustly.

Here the believer must be careful not to surrender to emotional blackmail. One response would be: "You suggest that it is fine to kill innocent children. The law says it is permissible to take the life of those who have committed capital crimes, been tried by a jury of their peers, and been given the presumption of innocence. If only our unborn children could again be given the same rights they enjoyed for almost 200 years, before Roe vs. Wade."

The *ad populum* (to the people)

Ask any teenager, and he will say, "Everyone is wearing. . . No one would be caught dead in. . . ." The *ad populum* fallacy is an appeal to popularity: everyone knows, everyone feels, or conversely, no one else shares your opinion. The popularity of an idea does not support or detract from its veracity. George Bernard Shaw, a pioneering socialist, said that we never tire of honoring live conformists and dead non-conformists.

This fallacy can be attacked by questioning the facts, such as when a church official said, "You and Jerry are the only ones who feel this way about Lutherans Concerned." This apparent aberration was tested subsequently by a resolution on the issue, where the confessional position earned more than two votes, though not many more. The real message of the *ad populum*, which is effectively destroying the mainline churches, is this: "You are not moving with the tide of change. You are not on the cutting edge of theology."

The victim of the *ad populum* should say, "The issue is not whether everyone agrees but whether this is right or wrong, according to the word of God." If the apostate attacks the Scriptures in front of an audience, he may experience a profound lack of support.

The *ad verecundiam* (out of respect)

Claiming authority for a statement is common and necessary in theology. False claims of authority, in contrast, are a logical fallacy. Luther and Calvin have been victimized by the false claims of mainline theologians, who commonly assert, without citations, that both reformers rejected the inerrancy of Scripture, that both were "free and creative" with the Bible, that both distinguished between the word of God and the Scriptures.

Martin Marty, the prolific Evangelical Lutheran Church in America pastor who teaches at the University of Chicago, pointed out in his Notre Dame summer lectures that a body of published work, even if it is wrong, establishes a "canon," a standard against which all future efforts are measured. Liberals have largely won the battle for control of American institutions by establishing in every area of thought a canon, a body of literature by accepted scholars.

We once stopped at a church-owned college to buy a Greek New Testament. The college bookstore and the student bookstore had no copies for sale, but both places had fifty separate titles about feminism and other recent causes. This church college serves as a source for many mainline seminary students. The canonical Scriptures have been replaced by the feminist/homosexual/Marxist/abortion canon, with obvious deleterious results for dogmatics. The alumni magazine of the college in question once featured articles about Christ, but recently honored a feminist advocate of abortion on demand and the main speaker at the homosexual convention in Toronto.

Countering an *ad verecundiam* fallacy can be tricky. Many mainline members are ill-informed about their own denomination's legacy of scholarship, considering it out of date. The best approach, then, is to appeal to their own authorities. Several liberal theologians, such as George Forell and Stanley Hauerwas, have opposed abortion on demand. *Christian Century,* a periodical of established liberalism, will occasionally publish an article questioning a prevailing myth, such as one about the crime of aborting a twin with Down's syndrome. Combating the *ad verecundiam,* then, requires a diet of liberal publications, or a reliable source of their latest intellectual follies.

The *ad ignorantiam* (pleading ignorance)

This particular fallacy is a natural for many people, because bad arguments require massive ignorance. However, the *argumentum ad ignorantiam* is a false plea, that something is true because it has not been shown to be false, that something is false because no one has proved it true. One mainline minister has repeatedly insisted that no one has ever proved the inerrancy of Scripture to him. One could cite the appropriate references in Pieper's *Christian Dogmatics*, Hoenecke's *Dogmatik*, and Robert Preus's *The Inspiration of Scripture*, but this fallacy provides a convenient cover: "You still haven't proved to me that the Bible claims to be inerrant."

The fallacy is widely used in books of liberal scholarship and in the classrooms of mainline schools. Some old warhorses of the Left:

1. No one can prove the Trinity from the Bible;
2. Paul never mentioned the virgin birth or the empty tomb;
3. Jesus did not claim to be the Messiah or the Son of God. For a college student untrained in Christian apologetics (the art of defending the faith), these statements can be devastating.

The fallacy of accidence

This false argument derives its name from the Latin word meaning "appearance." The fallacy of appearance consists of arguing from a general rule in dealing with an exceptional case. The converse fallacy of accidence means arguing from an exception for a general rule.

One denomination argued for abortion on demand by claiming correctly that Lutherans do not baptize dead babies. The general rule about the sacrament of baptism did not fit the ethics of killing a helpless child in the womb. The statement had the appearance of logic, but was fallacious and murderous. These are tricky to deal with, because a person with common sense knows something is wrong. A truth used in a misleading way is still dishonest.

Ignoratio elenchi (changing the subject)

The *ignoratio elenchi* consists of changing the subject, a time-honored method of avoiding the issue. In one discussion, a church leader was repeatedly asked if he favored the use of x-rated pornography in the treatment of sex offenders in church-sponsored programs. "Scripture has been understood from two perspectives. One is prescriptive. The other is descriptive." The issue was not hermeneutics but episcopal approval of pornography. He never answered the question.

The antidote to ignoratio elenchi is repeatedly saying, "Answer the question!"

Another form of the fallacy is using another question to deflect the original question. When a student was asked questions which threatened to expose his ignorance, he responded with this, "First, I want to ask about. . . ." The professor answered so thoroughly each time that he forgot his original question was unanswered. Questions, in whatever form they take, tend to control the direction of any conversation. A salesman and a debater will ask many questions.

Ad baculum (appeal to force)

A mainline minister was appointed to the Minnesota Council of Churches in time to consider a radical proposal endorsing homosexual rights. He did not attack the item but asked some clarifying questions. During a break another minister said, "What do you think you are doing? Do you want to be on this council or not?" The threat was clear enough: people who question the agenda do not stay on the council.

Another minister challenged the policies of the national youth board, which was sponsoring homosexual workshops for the teenagers. The responses varied, from "What is your hang-up?" (ad hominem) to "How badly do you want to be on the national staff?" (ad baculum). Unfortunately, many have succumbed to the threat of force, whether it is the loss of ministerial pension, the loss of church property, or the loss of a call. The answer is to fear God rather than man.

Ad misericordiam (sympathy)

A plea for sympathy (*ad misericordiam*) is often combined with special pleading for popular causes. For instance, a United Presbyterian minister said, "Here is a handicapped woman with no husband and no job. Are you going to insist that she must have a baby?" The special pleading (offering only reasons for an abortion) added to the intended effect of the multiple problems faced by the woman in question. In fact, many abortions are performed on married women with excellent health and with above average income, and some "terminations" are done solely to allow the couple to choose the sex of the child. The "wrong" sex is aborted.

A harsh answer to this mainline minister would have made the speaker seem heartless. (For instance, the pro-life speaker might say, "How did this handicapped woman get pregnant without being married?") Often people will identify with the distress of the single person. Instead of a harsh response, the speaker can switch to the language of the Presbyterian. "I'm pro-choice . . . that is, I will be pro-choice the moment we give unborn babies a choice in whether they live or die."

The *ad misericordiam* fallacy can be defeated by employing the Pauline method of using the opponents' terms against them. What is genuine compassion? According to one liberal minister, abortion on demand prevented children from being unwanted and therefore beaten. Someone responded, "Should we kill children to keep them from being beaten, to show our compassion?" The pro-abortion minister walked away without answering. Mainline ministers may have a monopoly on speaking about compassion, but not on compassion itself.

MATERIAL FALLACIES OF
INSUFFICIENT EVIDENCE

The following fallacies depend on their force from a lack of factual support. If the argument appeals to the prejudice of the audience, people will approve. A well-executed fallacy will leave supporters smiling and opponents baffled. Diagnosis is a crucial part of the cure.

Post Hoc, Ergo Propter Hoc (after this, therefore because of this)

The *post hoc* fallacy follows this pattern: When X happens, Y also happens; therefore X causes Y. These arguments were used to justify the introduction of the Social Gospel movement to mainline seminaries. The great depression (Y) happened after the excesses of capitalism had gone unchecked by the mainline churches (X), they argued. Since the mainline churches still preached individual salvation, that quietism caused the depression. Therefore, the church had to use its material and spiritual resources to reform society. The argument is based on unwarranted assumptions. First of all, the true cause of the depression was not the residual conservatism of the mainlines. The stock market crash was not the cause of the depression, either. The main cause was the imposition of a rigid tariff system, turning America's recession into a worldwide financial collapse.

To combat a post hoc fallacy, one must analyze the cause and the effect. The adverbs may be loosely used and vulnerable to attack. "Every time you drive, the car has another dent," The defense: "Every time? Yesterday? Last Monday? I drive it three times a week. It should have 347 dents in it by now." The question is really whether X caused Y, or whether X was the sole cause of Y.

Petitio principii (begging the question)

Begging the question is a simple or elaborate way of proving that X is true because X is true. One church executive, in attacking the traditional doctrine of inerrancy, said, "The terms inerrant and infallible are confusing because they offer less than they promise." One antidote to begging the question is a simple analysis of the statement. The believer might ask, "Aren't you using the conclusion to restate the argument, rather than proving it? Isn't that begging the question?"

Another way to stop this tactic is to profess confusion, dismay, or befuddlement. "What did you just say? It didn't make sense. Weren't you arguing in a circle?"

It is also fair to expect a claim to be supported by valid evidence rather than another version of the claim.

For that reason, orthodox Christians should be ready to give a "reason for the hope that is in you" (1 Peter 3:15), knowing that God always works through the Word, regardless of our abilities.

Opposition

The fallacy of opposition, designated by Carney and Scheer in *Fundamentals of Logic,* works this way: He is in favor of this, so we are opposed; or, he is opposed to this, so we are in favor of it. Hitler is a popular component of this argument. In the *Midland Daily News,* the liberal editor quoted someone's opposition to pornography, made a plea for free speech, then concluded the article by admitting in an ominous tone that Hitler had written the passage in question.

The implied conclusion was that people opposed to pornography were Nazis, or that we should protect the production of obscene material because of Hitler's statements against it. The fallacy was countered by identifying the lack of logic, quoting the textbook, and summarizing the tacky life of Hitler, citing *The Rise and Fall of the Third Reich,* a widely owned, if not widely read, book.

A common tirade offered up as truth starts in the following way: "The same people who oppose a woman's free choice are in favor of the military buildup." The implication is that opposition to abortion is not a genuine rejection of killing but a pretense, a hidden desire to oppress women in the name of the sanctity of life. It follows then that people should oppose the anti-abortion people as fiercely as they should oppose the defense industry.

The believer should seize the initiative as quickly as possible, pointing out that two issues are involved, abortion and defense, that many people of all political persuasions oppose abortion (rendering the grand conclusion false), that it is mischievous to make such hasty, arbitrary, and capricious statements. Another antidote is to ask why anyone would favor violent solutions, such as abortion, to social problems.

Special pleading

When only the arguments on one side of the issue are offered, without accounting for opposing views, the person is indulging in special pleading. When certain elements argued for legalized gambling in New Jersey, only the economic benefits were mentioned in an expensive media campaign. That was a clear case of special pleading.

When the mainline denominations changed their constitutions to allow women's ordination, they claimed it was only a matter of changing pronouns or establishing justice. By ignoring the relevant passages of Scripture, they engaged in special pleading.

The only answer to special pleading is a clear and logical presentation of the other side. In the case of the ordination of women, which is now a "women's issue," these facts would be germane in many denominations:

1. Scripture is our norm for faith and practice.
2. The pastoral epistles do not allow for the ordination of women or for women to exercise authority over men in the church.

3. Nearly twenty centuries of tradition should call into question the claims of women's ordination, especially when we see that women ruled most of Europe in the 16th century without anyone concluding at the time that women must preach as well.

Hasty generalization

Generalizations are not wrong, but it is a fallacy to argue that a general rule fits all those in that category. An interesting example was offered by a feminist minister in training, who had just summarily dismissed the virgin birth and the resurrection as "unimportant doctrines." She suggested that Christ could be understood as a woman because he compared himself to a mother hen! (This also represents a momentary lapse into Fundamentalism, an apostate becoming rabidly literal on one particular point.)

Mainline ministers enjoy telling horror stories about a particular conservative and then making a hasty generalization. Believers are also guilty of making a hasty generalization if they think all mainline seminary professors deny the virgin birth simply because it can be shown that most of them do. We are in contact with one mainline seminary professor who teaches the virgin birth without equivocation. Another hasty generalization made by some conservatives is that all ministers of mainline groups are unbelievers. If a believer states a hasty generalization as fact and one exception can be proven, the argument is blown to pieces.

Those mainline ministers who are more orthodox have been used as examples by their opponents of how tolerant the denomination is. "We have room for everyone, and we need your zeal." Precision of language is extremely important to avoid the charge of hasty generalization. The believer, by being well informed, can counter the hasty generalization by pointing out exceptions to brash claims.

FALLACIES OF AMBIGUITY

The following arguments depend on misuse of the language, as if we can use words to mean what we want them to mean at the moment, like the character in *Alice in Wonderland.*

Equivocation

Equivocation is the method of using the same word in two different senses. Liberal theology is essentially an equivocation at every point of doctrine, as witnessed by Adolph Harnack's *What Is Christianity?* and Walter Rauschenbusch's *A Theology for the Social Gospel.*_Countless examples can be found in mainline "confessions of faith," especially in respect to the Scriptures.

Equivocation is countered by demanding clear definitions of terms used. Blurred distinctions are used deliberately to confuse the unwary. The believer must say, "What do you mean by. . . ?" Because written materials can be misleading, the believer must discover how words are being used. Some efforts are rather transparent, such as when the Religious Coalition for Abortion Rights launched a campaign claiming that pro-abortion activists were pro-life, since they were concerned about the mother's life. Other attempts work quite well, such as the independent Lutheran congregation which called itself "Orthodox Lutheran" and yet borrowed, word for word, a statement of faith from the most liberal Lutheran group, a doctrinal summary which the national magazine claimed as a triumph of the historical-critical method.

Equivocations about moral issues come from equivocations about the faith. If a minister denies that the Bible is the revealed word of God, without any errors or contradictions, his moral reasoning will be deficient and misleading. His members will become confused by his leadership, the blind leading the blind.

Amphiboly

The term refers to an ambiguous sentence or group of sentences which allow two different conclusions to be drawn. Church bulletins are full of examples, such as the famous but apocryphal example of thanking the ladies' aid for laying Easter eggs on the altar. The Father of Lies could never afford to let his followers communicate directly and honestly about their theology and their causes. Funds would dry up. Executive positions would disappear. Many would need to seek gainful employment. Instead, public statements are designed to suggest one conclusion to camp-followers and a different conclusion to believers. For instance, when one denomination became too obvious about its support for the Marxists in Nicaragua, where the church was being persecuted by the heroes of the main-lines, one church executive said, "Yes, we confess a bias, a bias toward the poor."

When the mainline churches publish reports about their work in world missions, outreach, and world hunger, one might expect the conversion of pagans, evangelism in America, and providing food for the hungry to be the chief activities of those agencies. In fact, it would be a genuine miracle, in the biblical sense of the term, if such work dominated their departments. Since mainline executives use the term "mission" for social activism, most mainline members naively think of God's work being done.

Accordingly, Evangelicals in the United Methodist church had to organize their own independent world mission agency to get some genuine missionary work done. Were their bishops relieved and grateful? No, the United Methodist bishops boycotted the first commissioning service.

Accent

A fallacy of accent derives its error in placing the emphasis on the wrong element in the statement. For instance, a Lutheran layman called into question a prayer for the pope after the assassination attempt in 1981, wondering if the prayer implied doctrinal unity with Rome. The minister responded in the following way: "I apologize for showing concern." A solution is to question the accent. In this case, the issue was not of sympathy for the wounded pope but of doctrinal agreement. Instead of sarcasm, the minister could have explained, "I don't like church leaders shot down in public, even when we disagree with their confession of faith." The use of a fallacy made the minister appear evasive and defensive.

OTHER FALLACIES

Straw man

When an argument is weak, one is tempted to construct straw man fallacy. The straw man is a false construction of the opponent's views. The executive director of the Michigan Religious Coalition for Abortion Rights shouted into the phone, "What you want is to have every woman in America tested for pregnancy every month." The response which destroyed her straw man fallacy was a simple question about the facts: "Is that what happened before the 1973 decision, Roe vs. Wade?" A sputtering sound was heard.

The popularity of the straw man comes from the habit of bellowing arguments at those who agree with us. People are often convinced that the straw man fallacies they construct are the genuine views of the other side. An agency head said, "You're saying that. . . ." By calling attention to her straw man argument and naming it, the victim was able to stop the attack. Self-defense is hardly the answer. If the believer says, "I'm not saying . . . ," then the opponent can continue to press his attack.

Slippery slope

Advocates of pornography love the slippery slope. "If we censor this child pornography, even though I loathe its content, then we are just one step closer to a Nazi police state." Two matters are involved in the slippery slope. First, is this really a step toward the slope? Second, is the slope really so slippery? Banning child pornography is not a step toward censorship but a means of protecting the innocent. The constitution guarantees the free exercise of religion, not the free exercise of pornography.

Remember Viet Nam? Some people howled with laughter every time someone suggested that the loss of South Viet Nam would lead to the domination of Southeast Asia by the Communists. They complained that the domino theory was a slippery slope fallacy. The Soviets, who now use the crucial naval base we built in Viet Nam, thought otherwise.

Countering the slippery slope involves an examination of both premises.

False dilemma

A false dilemma proposes only two possibilities, both unsavory, to the listener. "If we do not allow for homosexual marriages, more social chaos will result from a lack of stability in their relationships." Several antidotes to this ancient falsehood are possible:

1. Attack one horn of the dilemma or the other;
2. Jump between the horns;
3. Construct a counter-dilemma.

Number one: Will homosexual marriage really foster stability? Our legal tradition suggests that unnatural relationships have never been endorsed by Western society, precisely because sanctifying wrong has a destabilizing effect on relationships of all kinds. Number two: Since more chaos is not desirable, we must return to the concept of natural law, which assumes universal principles of right and wrong based upon God as the creator. Number three: If we do legalize homosexual marriages, we will surrender the most basic foundation of morality, lead more people astray, and spread disease.

Two wrongs/common practice

Most people know that one wrong does not justify another, but all anti-Christian attitudes are based upon wrong and seek vindication through this falsehood. "Sex education may condone promiscuity, but isn't it better to teach them birth control than to have more illegitimate children born?" Conceding that birth control at the age of sixteen is wrong is followed by claiming that unwanted children are worse. One response would be to say, "Two wrongs don't make a right." Another would be to propose a solution, such as teaching deontological ethics (based on principles) rather than teleological ethics (the end justifying the means).

Common practice is related to two wrongs. "Everyone is doing it. It's common practice." Common practice is used to justify the use of illegal drugs, the theft of small items, the practice of deceit. One executive said, "The only question is—how much lying do you do?" The popularity of sin does not make it virtuous.

RULES OF ENGAGEMENT

Gilbert has offered these valuable "super-rules" for winning arguments: 1) Never give in; 2) Listen.[2] The first super-rule is a warning not to concede anything to an opponent, even while looking for concessions from him. Centuries ago Thomas Aquinas stated that one could not make progress in a debate unless the other person conceded some ground.

The second rule needs to be remembered in the heat of debate. We should not be so much in love with our own words that we fail to listen to the other person. In many cases, two people are saying the same thing in different ways.

However, if the opponent is a genuine, dedicated enemy of the Scriptures, listening for a weak point or a minor concession is essential. It is too easy to become emotional, an indication that the conversation is becoming personal. At that point, the issues have been sacrificed to personality. A confident person listens well and comes across as reasonable, articulate and temperate.

The following rules have been learned on the battlefield:

1. The best case is made by the person who remains calm, reasonable, friendly, and sincere. Wisconsin Synod pastors are unusually well trained in apologetics. One WELS pastor carefully explained the position of confessional Lutheranism while being taunted and baited by an unrepentant apostate. The liberal became red-faced with frustration while the Wisconsin Synod pastor remained calm. Who made the best impression?

2. Liberals seldom want to examine the issues closely, preferring to offer a dramatic enactment of some memorized fallacies. As Concordia, Ft. Wayne professor David Scaer has said, "Debating with liberals is like hunting cows with a bazooka."

3. Because liberals are such poor debaters, one should be careful to remember the audience. A well-known Evangelical destroyed a famous atheist in a public forum, making the unbeliever an object of sympathy.[3]

4. Ask questions, since questions control the discussion. Use "closing" questions, such as, "That would be the compassionate thing to do, wouldn't it?" or "You are not trying to say that all the Christian

ministers, laity, bishops, and theologians were wrong for centuries about the Bible being God's word, until Reimarus said otherwise, are you?"

5. The New Testament offers many examples of defending the faith, such as Paul, who never passed up an opportunity to evangelize. 1 Peter 3:15,16 RSV says:

> But sanctify the Lord God in your hearts,
> and always be ready to give a defense to
> everyone who asks you a reason for the hope
> that is in you, with meekness and with fear;
> having a good conscience, that when they
> defame you as evildoers, those who revile
> your good conduct in Christ may be
> ashamed.

6. The Word of God is always effective (Isaiah 55:11), so we should not shrink from debate because of a paralyzing sense of modesty.[4]
7. The truth is so compelling to people that some liberals will listen for hours while every one of their sacred cows is turned into hamburger.
8. Luther has said that Christ has already done everything for us. There is nothing for us to do except tell the good news to our neighbors.[5]

An active, living faith leads us to proclaim God's word wherever the opportunity arises, knowing the Holy Spirit will place the right words in our mouths. We will not always be successful. Paul sometimes failed to persuade, because of the hardness of his listeners' hearts, but Paul never ceased being faithful to the truth.

NOTES

1. My son, Martin, gave me invaluable help with this chapter. The categories of logical fallacies come from James Carney and Richard Scheer, *Fundamentals of Logic,* New York: Macmillan, 1964 . The book consistently makes liberal arguments seem logical while making a parody of traditional thinking. Another example of this is Michael Gilbert's *How To Win an Argument,* New York: McGraw-Hill, 1979. Both books are good mental exercises for the Christian apologist.

2. *How to Win an Argument.*

3. William A. Rusher has made this point in *How To Win Arguments,* Lanham, Maryland: University Press of America, 1981.

4. Three useful books on Christian apologetics are: Josh McDowell, *Evidence That Demands a Verdict,* 2 vols., San Bernardino: Here's Life Publishing, 1986; William Arndt, *Bible Difficulties and Seeming Contradictions,* St. Louis: Concordia Publishing House, 1987; Uuras Saarnivaara, *Can The Bible Be Trusted?* Minneapolis: Osterhus Publishing House, 1983.

5. Martin Luther, *Sermons of Martin Luther,* 6 volumes, Grand Rapids: Baker Book House; First Sunday after Easter. This is an excellent sermon on evangelism.

6.

THE CURE

The attack on the word of God which was once the sole ambition of only a few academic theologians in Europe has become a malignancy in America, one that threatens to overtake and destroy the vitality of the Christian faith. The malignancy has metastasized to such an extent that the victims of liberalism, ordinary church members, are sometimes found routinely reciting the speculations of Unitarian rationalism while innocently assuming they are correct interpretations of God's word. For instance, a participant in Pastor Robert Sauer's Missouri Synod adult class blandly "explained" the feeding of the five thousand by noting that the great generosity of the young boy made the multitude share their own lunches, yielding the remarkable amount of leftovers.[1] How tragic to see a believer innocently reciting the rationalistic interpretation of the Bible which began this era of apostasy!

A member of a Baptist church verbally attacked Rev. Jerry Falwell on Ted Koppel's TV show (May 12, 1988) for daring to believe that the Bible is infallible. The Baptist member confessed his doubt in the complete truth of the Scriptures. The image of Protestants whether Baptist, Methodist or Presbyterian—proclaiming only the truth of the Bible, has been shattered, providing disillusioned prospects for cults and the occult.

Lutherans resisted abandoning the Scriptures longer than the other denominations, doubtless because Lutheranism began with the re-establishment of Scripture alone. Yet today the vast majority of Lutherans in America are being taught by pastors who no longer believe, as Luther did, that the Bible has no errors or contradictions in it. Only the Wisconsin Evangelical Lutheran Synod, the Evangelical Lutheran Synod, the Church of the Lutheran Confession, and a few other small Lutheran groups consistently maintain a position once considered undebatable among Lutherans.

People have sought cures for the ills of their denominations. They have formed special caucuses and published special newsletters to alert people to the doctrinal and social issues. Even those groups founded to promote the inerrancy of the Scriptures have found themselves compromising on the very issue which initially galvanized their leaders and members. And, just like Andover Seminary, which was founded to protest the liberalism of Harvard, these groups end up as clones of their erstwhile opponents. Truly, all man-made cures must fail, since they bear with them the seed of their own destruction, a reliance upon human ability.

Fuller Seminary, founded in 1947 to maintain the inerrancy of Scriptures, furnishes one poignant example of human failure. The school began as a conscious alternative to Princeton Theological Seminary, which had split already in 1929 over inerrancy. The faculty and students involved in the 1929 split became leaders of the neo-Evangelical movement in the United States: J. Gresham Machen, Cornelius VanTil, Ned Stonehouse, and Harold J. Ockenga. Ockenga, minister of Park Street Church in Boston, was instrumental in founding Fuller Seminary and the magazine *Christianity Today*. Although the radio preacher Charles E. Fuller ("Old Fashioned Revival Hour") provided the money for a seminary which taught inerrancy, his son, Daniel P. Fuller, a student of Barth, moved the institution step-by-step to a position of errancy, which is the Barthian or neo-orthodox view of Scripture.

Fuller Seminary replayed the drama which every mainline seminary had already experienced. At first the liberal position on the Scriptures was not tolerated, so a moderate faculty member left Fuller by common consent. Next, a friend of the founder's son was hired as librarian, in spite of his position against inerrancy, but only if he did not teach. That restriction was dropped shortly. Then a president known for his opposition to inerrancy, David A. Hubbard, was hired. By 1962, the new position on the errancy of Scriptures was established at Fuller, yet the school continued to insist that the entire faculty held the position for which the school was founded.

When Harold Lindsell revealed "The Strange Case of Fuller Theological Seminary" in *The Battle for the Bible,* many Evangelicals denounced him for hurting the reputation of the seminary he helped establish but felt compelled to leave when its purpose was deliberately and methodically compromised.[2] Once this was accomplished, the Fuller School of Missions was begun in 1965, with Donald McGavran as dean. Through McGavran and his disciples at Fuller—Win Arn, John Wimber, and C. Peter Wagner—the Church Growth Movement has swept through most denominations in America, including the Lutheran groups.

Luther saw the flowering of the gospel during his own lifetime and experienced the same attacks upon the Scriptures which plague America today. He saw that people were looking for God everywhere except in the appointed means by which God chose to offer his grace to people: the word and the sacraments. To accomplish God's will, we must return to his plan, the word and the sacraments, relying on the Holy Spirit to work the will of God. What America lacks today is faithfulness to the Scriptures.

Conversion

Even in recent years, people have sought to improve the American religious scene by creating new institutions to advance scriptural inerrancy, or by seeking to take over those denominations where inerrancy was severely compromised. The failure of those efforts reminds us that the goal of God's word is not institutional but personal, showing us that he can indeed work through the weak and poor, even as he did when the Savior was born in poverty, shame, and weakness. Therefore we should not make power our goal, but seek to remain faithful to the whole counsel of God. Because God's will is that all people be saved, the gospel message of redemption from sin remains the central message of the church.

The power of historic Christianity has been a determined insistence upon the work of God alone in converting a person who is dead in sin and bestowing upon him a living faith in Christ Jesus as Lord and Savior, apart from any merit or cooperation in that person. At the same time, human reason has been at war against this gospel message, fueled by Satan's burning ambition to rob God of His glory and delude man into some palatable, reasonable, but insipid imitation of the gospel. C. F. W. Walther writes:

> Luther's remark about the enmity of all heretics against the grace of God is an important axiomatic statement. Every heresy that has sprung up was caused by the heretic's inability to believe that man becomes righteous in the sight of God, and is saved, by grace alone. That is the real rock of offense against which all heretics, all false teachers, dash their head.[3]

If we wander away from the tenets of grace alone, faith alone, Scripture alone, then the height of our steeples, the depth of our carpeting, and the yield on our endowments will mean nothing.

THE LAW

We know that God is perfect, upholding his perfect law.

> You are not a God who takes pleasure in evil;
> with you the wicked cannot dwell.
> The arrogant cannot stand in your presence;
> you hate all who do wrong.
> You destroy those who tell lies;
> bloodthirsty and deceitful men
> the LORD abhors. (Psalm 5:4-6 NIV)

When we rebel against the law, the law breaks our bones and crushes our arrogance. "The sacrifices of God are a broken spirit; a broken and contrite heart, O God, you will not despise." (Psalm 51:17 NIV)

All of the work of conversion takes place through the Holy Spirit. "The man without the Spirit does not accept the things that come from the Spirit of God, for they are foolishness to him, and he cannot understand them, because they are spiritually discerned" (1 Corinthians 2:14 NIV).

The childlike simplicity of Luther's Small Catechism describes the work of the Spirit:

> I believe that I cannot by my own thinking or choosing believe in Jesus Christ, my Lord, or come to him. But the Holy Spirit has called me by the gospel, enlightened me with his gifts, sanctified and kept me in the true faith. In the same way he calls, gathers, enlightens, and sanctifies the whole Christian church on

earth, and keeps it with Jesus Christ in the one true faith. . . .[4]

Here faith is not the result of the skillful evangelist who makes the Christian faith relevant by adding reason, nor is faith the accomplishment of the individual. Instead, it is the work of the Holy Spirit through the gospel. Hoenecke contrasts the scriptural position with that of the *Schwaermer* who dominate the American church scene:

> *Aus dem allen folgt die Verwerflichkeit des schwarmgeistlichen Grundsatzes, dass der Geist wirke ohne die Schrift. Geist nicht ohne Schrift, Schrift nicht ohne Geist, das ist gesunde Lehre.* (From this follows the repudiation of Pentecostal principle, that the Spirit works without the Scriptures. Spirit not without the Scripture, Scripture not without the Spirit— that is sound doctrine.) [5]

First of all, the unpopular but necessary work of preaching the law in all its severity must be undertaken. As Luther writes:

> Now God drives us to this by holding the law before us, in order that through the law we may come to a knowledge of ourselves. For where there is not this knowledge, one can never be saved. He that is well needs no physician; but if a man is sick and desires to become well, he must know that he is weak and sick, otherwise he cannot be helped. [6]

Knowing this to be true, C. F. W. Walther warns pastors:

> If remission of sins without repentance is preached, the people imagine that they have

already forgiveness of sins, and thereby they are
made secure and unconcerned. This is a greater
error and sin than all error of former times, and
it is verily to be feared that we are in that danger which Christ points out when He says,
Matthew 12:45: "The last state of that man shall
be worse than the first."[7]

Here we have an answer for the apparent bloom of
popular Christianity, without any lasting quality, TV
empires founded on greed, crumbling from the effects
of lust and corruption:

Unless the rocky subsoil in their hearts has
been pulverized by the law, the sweet gospel is
of no benefit to them.[8]

The preaching of the law is just as much the work of
the Holy Spirit as is the preaching of the gospel.
Luther wrote: "A penitent heart is a rare thing and a
great grace; one cannot produce it by thinking about
sin and hell. Only the Holy Spirit can impart it."[9]
While previous eras have been weighted down with
law preaching, due to the impact of Pietism, our era
is remiss in that area, due to the impact and the outward success of health and wealth theology. The
absence of law preaching is especially noteworthy
among those who have abandoned the overemphasis
of their tradition: Robert Schuller, who rejects the
negativism of Calvin; Norman V. Peale, who glibly
endorses universalism. Jim and Tammy Bakker
exchanged the drab poverty of Wesleyan holiness
Pentecostalism for a legendary lifestyle of make-up,
jewels, and luxury cars. The Bakkers' "Forgiven"
campaign has been followed by their grieved denials
of any significant wrongdoing. These leaders of
American Christianity come from the Reformed/
Pietistic tradition.

How easy it is for us to move from objective justification to the believer's apprehension of salvation through faith, without annoying him with details about God's perfect law, the sinfulness of popular social trends, or the necessity of repentance. Preaching the law to work repentance through the Holy Spirit in the hearts of people will continue to be the work of all gospel preachers, indeed, of all Christians. Luther commented: "True is the proverb and better than everything they have hitherto taught about remorse: Never to sin again is repentance at its best; and a new life is the best of repentance."[10]

THE GOSPEL

Nothing should make a Christian more confident in the work of evangelism than the assurance that God accomplishes everything through his word according to his pleasure:

> For you do not find Him; He finds you. For the preachers come from Him, not from you. . . . Your faith comes from Him, not from you. And everything that works faith within you comes from Him and not from you.[11]

This is the exact point where the Reformed, the Quakers, and the Pentecostals depart from Scripture. This is the heart of the Apostolic faith and the nemesis of all sects.

> For we can definitely assert that where the Lord's Supper, Baptism, and the word are found, Christ, the remission of sins, and life eternal are found. On the other hand, where these signs of grace are not found, or where they are despised by men, not only grace is

lacking but also foul errors will follow. Then men will set up other forms of worship and other signs for themselves.[12]

Pieper saw clearly what many Lutheran leaders overlooked in the past and continue to overlook today:

The history of dogma tells this story: In those doctrines in which it differs from the Lutheran Church and for the sake of which it has established itself as a separate body within visible Christendom, the Reformed Church, as far as it follows in the footsteps of Zwingli and Calvin, sets aside the Scripture principle and operates instead with rationalistic axioms. The Reformed theologians frankly state that reason must have a voice in determining Christian doctrine.[13]

In many places, Luther emphasized the power of God instead of the works of man. He wrote about John 21:19-24:

Firstly, we read that this was the disciple whom Christ loved. This means that faith alone makes the truly beloved disciples of Christ, who receive the Holy Spirit through this very same faith, not through their works. Works indeed also make disciples, but not beloved disciples: only temporary hypocrites who do not persevere. God's love does not uphold and keep them, for the reason that they do not believe.[14]

In a sermon on John 6:43-44, he reiterated this message of grace:

Christ here says: Only he comes to Me and only he receives faith whom the Father draws to Me. This drawing is not done as the hangman draws a thief. It is rather a friendly inviting and drawing, as a gracious man attracts people to himself by being so friendly and pleasant that everybody is glad to go to him. In this way God also gently invites and brings people to Himself so that they willingly and gladly are with Him and near Him. [15]

Thus we see the compelling force of Luther's Gospel, an eloquence radiating from God's glory rather than from man's wisdom. Unfortunately, many people do not understand the enmity of the Protestant sects toward the means of grace. I have experienced this firsthand on several occasions. In one case, a Pentecostal woman ran from the room crying when a Lutheran pastor talked about infant baptism at a Lutheran retreat. Later, when I discussed infant baptism with a group of people, at their invitation, a member of the Assemblies of God glared at me, furious about my opportunity to teach them, even though I discussed both sides fairly and without polemics. At Wheaton College, at the Billy Graham Center, in the Cliff Barrows Auditorium, I discussed the same issue with a Baptist minister, who brought it up when I admitted to being a Lutheran pastor. When I pointed out that his practice of infant dedication was a tacit concession to the scriptural position, he broke off the conversation he had started. In short, the sectarians are well trained against the means of grace, and this principled opposition lies at the heart of decision theology, Church Growth methods, and Pentecostalism.

Some people think it is not fair to cite Zwingli as the well-spring of sectarian opposition to the Means of Grace. Moderate Lutherans and Calvinists plead that Calvin came closest to Luther. In fact, some of Calvin's statements can sound quite appealing to a Lutheran:

Wherever we see the Word of God purely preached and heard, and the sacraments administered according to Christ's institution, there, it is not to be doubted, a church of God exists.[16]

But Calvin can also be quite appalling, separating the means of grace from the Holy Spirit, just as he separated the two natures of Christ:

The nature of baptism or the Supper must not be tied down to an instant of time. God, whenever He sees fit, fulfills and exhibits in immediate effect that which He figures in the sacrament. But no necessity must be imagined so as to prevent His grace from sometimes preceding, sometimes following, the use of the sign.[17]

Calvin clearly divorced the Holy Spirit from the means of grace:

But the sacraments properly fulfill their office only when the Spirit, that inward teacher, comes to them, by whose power alone hearts are penetrated and affections moved and our souls opened for the sacraments to enter in. If the Spirit be lacking, the sacraments can accomplish nothing more in our minds than the splendor of the sun shining upon blind eyes, or a voice sounding in deaf ears.[18]

Although the Reformed will use the word sacrament, the actual meaning of the term reflects Calvin's exegesis:

We must establish such a presence of Christ in the supper as may neither fasten Him to the element of bread, nor enclose Him in bread, nor circumscribe Him in any way (all of which clearly derogate from His heavenly glory. . . .)[19]

Left unexplained by Calvin is how the church misunderstood for almost 16 centuries the Real Presence of the body and blood of Christ and the clear words of Holy Scripture: "This is my body."

THE WORD AND REASON

If we examine the relationship of the word to conversion, the differences between historic Christianity and sectarian Protestantism become even plainer. Luther taught that the word of God does not require the addition of human reason to make it relevant or effective. In contrast, Calvin insisted that human reason must be added, rejecting *nuda scriptura*. At the Chicago inerrancy conference in December of 1986, I witnessed two prominent Reformed theologians tongue-lash Dr. Robert Preus for adhering to *nuda scriptura*.[20] Adding human reason to Scripture has been the hallmark of sectarian Protestants, as Pieper notes:

> Reformed theologians, in order to support their denial of the *illocalis modus subsistendi* of Christ's human nature, have sought, in their exposition of John 20, an opening in the closed doors, or a window, or an aperture in the roof or in the walls, in order to explain the possibility of Christ's appearance in the room where the disciples were assembled.[21]

The great sectarian error is not one of magisterial reason in contrast to ministerial reason, for the Reformed, Pentecostal, and Baptist turn out in greater numbers than the Lutherans at inerrancy conferences.[22] The question is not of placing reason above the Word of God, but beside it, in partnership with it, similar to the Roman Catholic doctrine of Mary serving as Co-Redemptrix with Christ.

Pieper has written:

> Moved by rationalistic considerations, the
> Reformed reject Baptism and the Lord's Supper
> as means of grace; and some of them, in harmo-
> ny with their principle, have rejected the exter-
> nal Word of the Gospel as a means of grace and
> substituted for it an alleged 'immediate inner
> illumination,' and then have fallen into outright
> rationalism.[23]

The key word "effective," which shows up in sectarian evangelism material, is directly related to this false
doctrine. Luther cautions us:

> We must, therefore, be careful not to want to
> uphold the Gospel with our powers instead of
> with its own might. In that case it is entirely
> lost; and when one wants to defend it most effec-
> tively, it comes to naught. Let us shed all worry
> about the progress of the Gospel. The Gospel
> does not need our help. It is mighty enough by
> itself. Commit it to that God alone to whom it
> belongs.[24]

If reason must be added to the word of God to make
it effective, then the word of God alone is ineffective,
quite the opposite of the clear witness of Scripture:

> As the rain and the snow
> come down from heaven,
> and do not return to it
> without watering the earth
> and making it bud and flourish,
> so that it yields seed for the sower
> and bread for the eater,
> so is my word that goes out from my mouth:
> It will not return to me empty,

but will accomplish what I desire
and achieve the purpose for which I sent it.
(Isaiah 55:10,11 NIV)

Against the notion of a footloose working of the Holy Spirit, Luther states:

> One must not reverse the order and dream of a Holy Spirit who works without the Word and before the Word, but one who comes with and through the Word and goes no farther than the Word goes.[25]

Luther also advises us:

> From this it follows that they act foolishly, yea, against God's order and institution, who despise and reject the external Word, thinking that the Holy Spirit and faith should come to them without means. It will indeed be a long time before that will happen.[26]

> Whoever now believes the Gospel will receive grace and the Holy Spirit. This will cause the heart to rejoice and find delight in God, and will enable the believer to keep the law cheerfully, without expecting a reward, without fear of punishment, without seeking compensation, as the heart is perfectly satisfied with God's grace, by which the law has been fulfilled.[27]

EVANGELISM

Many Lutherans in America are suffering from a complete misapprehension of how the Holy Spirit works through the means of grace to convert people to a living faith. On the liberal side, evangelism is seen as

149

membership recruitment. Even among pastors there is a profound sense of embarrassment when talking about the Christian faith, though other matters can be discussed in clinical detail without a blush. To some extent, liberal Lutheran church leaders have been attracted to demographic studies, sociological trends, and marketing techniques.

Oddly enough, some conservative Lutheran pastors have been attracted to sectarian evangelism methods. Pastors and congregations are easily swindled by that old whore Reason into figuring how well they are doing in terms of numerical growth and financial success. Using such yardsticks, the Mormons are the ones truly blessed by God. In contrast, if we listen to Luther, Walther, Pieper, and Hoenecke, we will proclaim the gospel with confidence, confidence in God, not ourselves.

PIETISM

The sectarian denial of the means of grace should be clear to anyone who has read Luther, Pieper, or Calvin. However, while the sects are merely silent about the only genuine cause of church growth, the means of grace, they are quite voluble about their own methods. These methods are the substance of Pietism and are at war against the article on which the church stands or falls—justification by faith. The methods are: unionism; judging the results (or emphasizing fruit rather than doctrine); and *collegia pietatis* (cell groups). Some people might want to soft-pedal this issue, or avoid it altogether, but they should not invoke Luther's name to support their timidity. The Reformer tells us:

> Christendom must have men who are able to floor their adversaries and take armor and equipment from the devil, putting him to shame. But this calls for strong warriors who

have complete control of Scripture, can refute a false interpretation, know how to wrest the sword they wield, that is, their Bible passages, from the hands of the adversaries and beat them back with them.[28]

For every sect has always had one or more particular hobbies and articles which are manifestly wrong and can easily be discerned to be of the devil, who publicly teach, urge and defend them as right certain and necessary to believe or to keep. For the spirit of lies cannot so conceal himself but that he must at last put forth his claws, by which you can discern and observe the ravenous wolf.[29]

Unionism

Unionism, which is often called ecumenism, is the practice of establishing or expressing unity without a common confession of faith. Whenever Lutherans have been forced into a church union with the Reformed or entered a union agreement voluntarily, Lutherans have had to concede key doctrinal positions, especially the Real Presence of the body and blood of Christ in Holy Communion and baptismal regeneration, both of which are clearly taught in the Scriptures. Unionism has always created doctrinal indifference, and doctrinal indifference has always promoted unionism. First the Lutheran confessions are conceded, then the Scriptures themselves. Theodore Schmauk, who struggled against the anti-confessional spirit of the last century, predicted this in 1905:

The modern radical spirit which would sweep away the Formula of Concord as a Confession of the Church, will not, in the end, be curbed, until it has swept away the Augsburg Confession, and the ancient Confessions of the

Church—yea, not until it has crossed the borders of Scripture itself, and swept out of the Word whatsoever is not in accord with its own critical mode of thinking. The far-sighted rationalist theologian and Dresden Court preacher, Ammon, grasped the logic of a mere spirit of progress, when he said: 'Experience teaches us that those who reject a Creed, will speedily reject the Scriptures themselves.'[30]

The American religious scene has been dominated by Reformed theology from the beginning, starting with the Pilgrims who landed at Plymouth Rock in 1620, and continuing with the growth of Baptist, Methodist, and Pentecostal churches during the age of western expansion and revivalism. While the Protestant sects do not agree on many points of doctrine, they share a common origin: Zwingli's and Calvin's rejection of the means of grace. All non-Lutheran Protestants, whether Mennonite, Anglican, Baptist, Presbyterian, Methodist, or Pentecostal, agree in rejecting baptismal regeneration and the Real Presence. They also agree in many ways in their emphasis on sanctification or the Christian life.

Because Reformed theology, from Zwingli and Calvin, took away objective certainty in salvation through the means of grace, they necessarily substituted subjective criteria, the feeling of being saved, and outward signs, such as membership in cell groups. Essentially, Reformed theology created Pietism, influencing key Lutherans.

We should not be surprised that Philip Jacob Spener, the founder of Pietism, is considered by Heick the first union theologian. Spener rejected the Real Presence and baptismal regeneration, but accepted chiliasm. Spener was the first Lutheran theologian to include theological errors among those covered by the forgiveness of sins.[31]

The Evangelical institutions, whether the Billy Graham Evangelistic Association or *Christianity Today* or Fuller Seminary, have been unionistic from the beginning. The result has been a compromising position on inerrancy, first on inerrancy itself, then on basic doctrines of the Bible. Many people today see the modern Evangelical movement, which Harold Ockenga initiated in his 1948 convocation speech in Pasadena, as being completely rudderless, driven by the wind, tossed back and forth, having no clear position on any doctrine of the Bible.

Therefore, one aspect of the cure is to avoid unionism, which has always led to apostasy, and continue to maintain the scriptural principles of fellowship.

Results! Results!

The unionistic Evangelicals cannot deal with doctrinal matters so they concentrate on results, with a simple-minded formula—if something works, that is, adds to the visible church, it must be God-pleasing. This is paying obeisance to the era of Pietism, which Walther criticized:

> 'Pay more attention to pure life, and you will raise a growth of genuine Christianity.' That is exactly like saying to a farmer: 'Do not worry forever about good seed; worry about good fruits.' Is not a farmer properly concerned about good fruit when he is solicitous about getting good seed? Just so a concern about pure doctrine is the proper concern about genuine Christianity and a sincere Christian life. False doctrine is noxious seed, sown by the enemy to produce a progeny of wickedness. The pure doctrine is wheat-seed; from it spring the children of the Kingdom, who even in the present life belong in the kingdom of Jesus Christ, and in the life to come will be received into the Kingdom of Glory.[32]

Our experience in Ohio, a tiny minority of orthodox Lutherans offering an unpalatable way of life, was not unknown to Luther.

> Be not worried because of this! For even though a man preach and continue in the Gospel for many years, he must still lament and say: Aye, no one will come, and all continue in their former state. Therefore you must not let that grieve or terrify you.[33]

Some pastors may be tempted to feel that they have not made the gospel appealing or relevant to church shoppers of the Me Generation. Knowing that conversion did not depend upon man, Luther wrote:

> What business is it of mine that many do not esteem it? It must be that many are called but few are chosen. For the sake of the good ground that brings forth fruit with patience, the seed must also fall fruitless by the wayside, on the rock and among the thorns; inasmuch as we are assured that the Word of God does not go forth without bearing some fruit, but it always finds also good ground; as Christ says here, some seed of the sower falls also into good ground and not only by the wayside, among the thorns and on stony ground. For wherever the Gospel goes you will find Christians. 'My Word shall not return unto me void' (Isaiah 55:11).[34]

> Yet this is also true, that Christ often delays the bestowal of His help, as He did on this occasion, and on another, John 21, when He permitted the disciples to toil all the night without taking anything, and really appeared as if He would forget His own Word and promise.[35]

The pietistic basis for the modern Evangelicals is utter nonsense, as Walther proves with this Luther quotation:

> Now it is evident that fruits do not bear the tree, nor does the tree grow on the fruit, but the reverse—trees bear fruits, and fruits grow on trees. As there must be trees before there can be fruits, and as the fruits do not make the tree either good or corrupt, but the tree produces the fruits, even so man must first be either good or corrupt before he does good or corrupt works. His works do not make him either good or corrupt, but he does either good or corrupt works.[36]

Cell Groups

The origin of the cell group is, once again, the era of Pietism, where Spener urged and organized the prayer and Bible study groups to inculcate "deep-toned piety," as the Franckean Synod once called it. The weakness of this approach is the distinction, then, between various levels of Christianity, the goal or promise of creating a higher, deeper, or better form of the faith. Heick has explained why Pietism is at odds with orthodoxy:

> While Orthodoxy conceived of regeneration objectively as coinciding with baptism, pietism equated regeneration with conversion, conceiving of it as a subjective change in man. *The doctrine of baptismal regeneration, ardently defended by the Orthodox theologians, was rejected by the Pietists.* Regeneration is not complete, they taught, until the baptized responds to the promise of God with repentance and faith. Divine sonship is contingent upon conversion; only believers are sons of God.[37]

Modern Evangelicals urge the creation of "disciples," one of their favorite terms, and "soul-winners," through various pietistic techniques. Walther, very much affected by his sojourn with Pietists, describes three of their leaders (Francke, Breithaupt, Fresenius):

> These men were guilty of that more refined way of confounding Law and Gospel. They did this by making a false distinction between spiritual awakening and conversion; for they declared that, as regards the way of obtaining salvation, all men must be divided into three classes:
> 1. those still unconverted;
> 2. those who have been awakened, but are not yet converted;
> 3. those who have been converted.[38]

Hoenecke states how Pietism misleads people into accepting it as compatible with Lutheranism:

> *Wohl scheint auf den ersten Blick die ganze Differenz recht unbedeutend; aber in Wahrheit gibt sich hier die gefaehrliche Richtung der Pietisten zu erkennen, das Leben ueber die Lehre, die Heiligung ueber die Rechtfertigung und die Froemmigkeit nicht als Folge, sondern als Bedingung der Erleuchtung zu setzen, also eine Art Synergismus und Pelagianismus einzufuehren.* (At first glance, the total difference seems absolutely insignificant, but in truth the dangerous direction of Pietism is made apparent: life over doctrine, sanctification over justification, and piety not as a consequence but declared as a stipulation of enlightenment, accordingly leading to a kind of synergism and Pelagianism.) [39]

APPLICATION

Luther can tell us the bad and the good effects of the Evangelical sects:

> When one heresy dies, another presently springs up; for the devil neither slumbers nor sleeps. I myself—though I am nothing—who have now been in the ministry of Christ for twenty years, can truthfully testify that I have been attacked by more than twenty sects. Some of these have entirely perished; others still twitch with life like pieces of dismembered insects. But Satan, that god of factious men, raises up new sects.[40]

> But now these sects are our whetstones and polishers; they whet and grind our faith and doctrine so that, smooth and clean, they sparkle as a mirror. Moreover we also learn to know the devil and his thoughts and become prepared to fight against him.[41]

The time has come for all orthodox Christians to repudiate modern Evangelicalism, to carry out the scriptural admonition to "observe and avoid those who cause fatal errors"(Romans 16:17, author's translation). Francis Pieper warns us:

> Hence indifferentism here is surely not in place. On the contrary, we must challenge the teaching of any operation of the Spirit independently of the Word within the Christian Church, and combat it as a foreign element that has penetrated into the Christian doctrine and as a deadly enemy of living personal faith.[42]

Evangelism methods borrowed from Reformed, Quaker, and Pentecostal theologians cannot possibly be doctrinally neutral. This is supported by Luther:

> In philosophy an error that is small at the beginning becomes very great in the end. So a small error in theology overturns the whole body of doctrine. . . .That is why we may not surrender or change even an iota (*apiculum*) of doctrine.[43]

Modern Evangelicals would like us to learn their methods, and keep our confession of faith, that is, to be as indifferent as they are about doctrine. But Luther could not agree with such backpedaling:

> Doctrine is our only light. It alone enlightens and directs us and shows us the way to heaven. If it is shaken in one quarter *(in una parte)*, it will necessarily be shaken in its entirety *(in totum)*. Where that happens, love cannot help us at all.[44]

> In matters concerning faith we must be invincible, unbending, and very stubborn; indeed, if possible, harder than adamant. But in matters concerning love we should be softer and more pliant than any reed and leaf and should gladly accommodate ourselves to everything.[45]

Orthodox Lutherans may feel alone and envious in their small churches, especially in those places where their faithfulness is needed most. They can look around and see that the liberals and Evangelicals have built huge churches which dwarf their own. They may feel like failures, especially the pastors. But Walther, quoting Luther, has this to say to each and every pastor:

> Now, the Lord in this passage speaks, in particular, of preachers or prophets, whose real and

proper fruit is nothing else than this, that they diligently proclaim this will of God to the people and teach them that God is gracious and merciful and has no pleasure in the death of a sinner, but wants him to live, moreover, that God has manifested His mercy by having His only-begotten Son become man. After this fruit, which is the principal and most reliable one and cannot deceive, there follow in the course of time other fruits, namely, a life in beautiful harmony with this doctrine and in no way contrary to it. But these fruits are to be regarded as genuine fruits only where the first fruit, namely, the doctrine of Christ, already exists.[46]

The poison which has disabled American Christianity is false doctrine, introduced in small doses. The cure is not ours, but God's pure doctrine from the inerrant word of God. Each Christian has a role, however humble it may seem, in God's Kingdom, as Luther wrote:

And yet, one single Christian believer, by his preaching and prayer, can be the means of salvation to uncounted multitudes. In spite of Satan's hatred and desire to hinder, many people hear the Gospel, receive baptism and become teachers of the faith; and through the influence of the Gospel the sacredness of home and country are preserved.[47]

God keep us steadfast in his word.

A NEW APPROACH

The history of Lutheranism, ever since Luther died, and even before, is so discouraging to read that one is tempted to believe that God himself opposed the

Reformation from the very beginning. Luther's trusted co-worker, Philip Melanchthon, began to undo the Augsburg Confession a few years after it was written and later wavered in the face of opposition from Roman Catholics. Various leaders who drew their initial insights from Luther sought to impose their unique views upon Scripture. Not only were the Protestants divided, but even Lutherans fell to bickering among themselves instead of confessing together the truth of God's word. As a result, the Book of Concord had to be written to end the discord among the Lutheran factions.

In the following years, Lutherans faced determined opposition from the followers of Zwingli and Calvin, as well as from the Church of Rome. Dabblers in church history have been quick to portray Lutheranism as a middle course between the Medieval rituals of Rome and the gospel-centered preaching of the Protestants. This moderating position seems to be enhanced by the Roman view of Lutherans as too Protestant, by the Protestant view of Lutheranism as too Roman.

The mistaken view of Lutherans is derived from the degeneration of the visible church in the centuries following her establishment by Christ and the apostles. The church was created by and built upon the word of God. The sacraments of baptism and communion cannot be separated from the word, because the earthly elements of the sacraments derive their power from the word, just as iron alone cannot start a fire unless heated. The word is the power of the sacraments, just like the glow in the iron. The Zwinglians, Calvinists, and Pentecostals refuse to believe that the Holy Spirit works with the word and the earthly elements of the sacraments.

The Medieval church lost the power of the word, while retaining a distorted view of the sacraments. The image most people have of Catholicism comes from the Medieval errors which were codified and preserved by Rome at the Council of Trent, which met from 1545 to 1563. Although the Council of Trent is normally presented as the Counter-Reformation, a cleansing of corrupt practices, it really meant that the worst errors of the past would be the foundation of all future Roman teaching. At the center of the Reformation and the Counter-Reformation was the battle for the gospel itself, for the authority and clarity of the Scriptures. Luther battled for the scriptural doctrine of salvation through faith, apart from the works of the law, while Rome chose to continue the system of works and indulgences, purgatory, and masses for the dead. Thus Luther's work was not a revolution itself, though it seemed to be radical in contrast to the corrupt state of affairs, but a conservative Reformation, honoring the past where the foundations were sound.

Luther's student, Martin Chemnitz, proved in *The Examination of the Council of Trent*, with a careful study of the Scriptures and the Church Fathers, that Lutheranism was nothing more than the teaching and practice of the church's first centuries. While Luther made it impossible for Rome to appeal to Scripture, Chemnitz made it just as difficult to appeal to Jerome, Augustine, and Ambrose. Although Lutherans are not Roman Catholics, we are truly catholic, tracing our doctrine back through the centuries to the martyrs and saints who first stood for the truth and, in many cases, died for the word.

Tragically, Lutherans have been drawn from their catholic heritage by identifying with the Zwinglian and Pentecostal sects which first attacked Luther for maintaining what no one doubted in the previous sixteen centuries. While the Protestant sects taught the inerrancy of the Scriptures until rationalism took hold of the various denominations, they never taught that God gives rebirth through baptism or that the body and blood of Christ are truly present in the elements of communion.

In one Baptist seminary, the church history course starts with the apostles, then begins again with the

Reformation, as if the intervening fifteen centuries were of no consequence. Lutherans, in their fear of Romanism, have often been unafraid of sectarian Protestantism, adopting the worship, the robes, and even the doctrine of those whom Luther tried in vain to teach from Scripture. R. C. H. Lenski, published by the ELCA but almost unread in the ELCA, admonished an earlier audience of Lutherans who envied in their age the growth of the sectarians:

> Paul offers no excuse for preachers who desire to eliminate certain teachings of the gospel on the plea that they can thus reach and attract more people than if they insisted also on these teachings. Paul intends to omit, even in his own mind, any addition to the gospel, any admixture, any sugar-coating of it by human, worldly wisdom. [Text: "For I decided not to know anything among you save Jesus Christ, and him crucified" 1 Corinthians 2:2.][48]

If we measure success by numbers rather than by purity of doctrine, then the Scriptures must be altered, diluted, and perverted to have the greatest possible appeal at the moment. The smallest points of doctrine will grow in significance, as Lutherans wander away from the truth in search of error's success.

The power of the word of God, which the sectarians cannot understand, comes from the word alone. We do not need to make the word reasonable, appealing, or relevant. The Trinity, incarnation, virgin birth, atonement, and resurrection of Christ are beyond human reason, absurd to the world, yet transcending everything the world can imagine. Adding reason to the word, the fundamental weakness of Roman Catholicism and sectarians alike, must eventually yield to placing reason above the word. The saying is true, as

C. P. Krauth said, "Young Arminian, old Socinian". In other words, the person who adds reason to the word in his youth will become a Unitarian in his old age. Every denomination which has given reason a place along with Scripture has succumbed to Unitarianism as well, from the Reformed, who formerly taught inerrancy, to the Roman Catholics, who once condemned evolution and the historical-critical method of studying Scripture.

The weakness of adding reason to the Word is revealed in the latter stages of degeneration. The Word is God-centered, but reason is me-centered. God does not abide any idols in the human heart. Reason starts with the self and ends with the self, unless brought under submission by the word. Even then, the battle is never won completely. We can tie up a pig ever so tightly, but we cannot keep it from squealing, as Luther said.[49]

We should view ourselves as catholic in doctrine and worship because the faith of historic Christianity has been God-centered rather than me-centered, universal rather than parochial. In honoring the faithful witness of past leaders, we honor God's work in such people as Adolph Hoenecke, C. F. W. Walther, Martin Chemnitz, Martin Luther, John Hus, Augustine, Athanasius and Justin Martyr. We should study the orthodox dogmaticians of the past—Chemnitz, Selnecker, Gerhard, Calov, Quenstedt—because they were primarily students and teachers of the Word, as Robert Preus has shown.[50]

We should study the Lutheran Confessions and use them diligently in our growth as Christians, not because they are another Bible, but because they show us the disorders of the past, and the cure, which is the proper understanding of God's word.

Many cures of the past have started with action plans, goals, and objectives. Many church leaders have said to one another, when trying to adopt a secular fad,

"How can we baptize this concept and use it in the church?" only to wonder years later why the newest trend failed them so utterly. Many church members have joined a movement in good faith, for the good of the church, only to find the movement in a continuing state of flux and confusion.

By placing our faith in the word and sacraments, knowing that "God gives the growth," our self-confidence diminishes and our confidence in God grows. No one can reject us, so how can we fail to take the message of the gospel everywhere? People will hear the gospel, and the word will open their hearts, just as it opened the heart of Lydia: "As she listened, the Lord opened her heart to accept what Paul said" (Acts 16:14 NET). If they reject the word, they are rejecting Christ, not us.

Knowing that the strength of the church comes from the means of grace, we need not be ashamed of the pure doctrine of Scripture, or catholic worship using the historic liturgy, or the sacraments. We should heed God's warning to the Israelites, after they conquered Canaan:

> . . . Be careful not to be ensnared by inquiring about their gods, saying, "How do these nations serve their gods? We will do the same." You must not worship the Lord your God in their way, because in worshiping their gods, they do all kinds of detestable things the Lord hates (Deut. 12:30b-31a, NIV).

How strange that Lutherans would even consider aping the worship of those who deny the means of grace, who deny baptismal regeneration, who deny that Jesus Christ really meant, "This is my body!" We should not worry about convincing the world that we are friendly, that our nursery will take the worry out of being a parent, or that our church has something for every age group and hobbyist. We should simply tell them the truth, if we want to remain orthodox Lutherans: that we still teach what Luther taught, and that he taught what the church catholic once taught, as handed down from Christ and the apostles, and preserved by the fathers of the church.

Instead of trying to say that we are just like everyone else, when we are not, we can define ourselves boldly as a small minority of Lutherans in the world, only 5% of Lutherans in America: orthodox. One Jewish lawyer reacted to "Lutheran orthodoxy" with a half-hour discussion about doctrine and a desire to remain on the mailing list of a Wisconsin Synod congregation. His son died of Tay- Sachs, the degenerative disease which afflicts some Jews. A Jewish doctor responded to "Lutheran orthodoxy" by asking, with a smile, "Do you eat kosher?" He was delighted with the answer, "No, we read kosher." His only son died in an accident. Conversations with the physician have involved the Messiah, eternal life, and bearing the cross. Neither father would have been interested in a World War II discussion group.

The cure, which is the Holy Spirit, working through the word and sacraments, does not require more talent, more persuasive speech, better graphics, a laser printer, or more attractive pastors. What the world loves, God despises. What God loves, the world hates. God wants us to cling to the Holy Scriptures, the infallible revelation of his mighty deeds, from the six-day creation to the raising of the dead when Christ returns on the last day. The world adores success, but God honors faithfulness, lifting up the weakest of the weak,—Gideon, Deborah, David, Mary, Paul—to reveal his power, to show that his grace is sufficient. The closing statement of the Formula of Concord expresses with simple eloquence what it means to be a confessing Christian:

We have no intention of yielding aught of the eternal, immutable truth of God for the sake of temporal peace, tranquility and unity (which, moreover, is not in our power to do). Nor would such peace and unity, since it is devised against the truth and for its suppression, have any permanency. Still less are we inclined to adorn and conceal a corruption of the pure doctrine and manifest, condemned errors. But we entertain heartfelt pleasure and love for, and are on our part sincerely inclined and anxious to advance, that unity according to our utmost power, by which His glory remains to God uninjured, nothing of the divine truth of the Holy gospel is surrendered, no room is given to the least error, poor sinners are brought to true, genuine repentance, raised up by faith, confirmed in new obedience and thus justified and eternally saved alone through the sole merit of Christ.[51]

NOTES

1. Gregory L. Jackson, "Free Conference at Concordia, Ft. Wayne: ELCA, LCMS, WELS," *Christian News,* May 23, 1988, p. 1.
2. Harold Lindsell, *The Battle for the Bible,* Grand Rapids: Zondervan, 1976.
3. *The Proper Distinction Between Law and Gospel,* ed., W. H. T. Dau, St. Louis: Concordia Publishing House, 1928, p. 163.
4. *What Luther Says, An Anthology,* 3 vols., St. Louis: Concordia Publishing House, I, p. 353.
5. Adolf Hoenecke, *Evangelische-Lutherische Dogmatik,* 4 vols., Milwaukee: Northwestern Publishing House, IV, p. 17.
6. Martin Luther, *The Sermons of Martin Luther,* 8 vols., Grand Rapids: Baker Book House, II, p. 370.
7. Walther, p. 123.
8. *Ibid.,* p. 119.
9. *What Luther Says,* III, p. 1212.
10. *What Luther Says,* III, p. 1214.
11. *What Luther Says,* I, p. 345.
12. *What Luther Says,* II, p. 914.
13. Francis Pieper, *Christian Dogmatics,* 3 vols., St. Louis: Concordia Publishing House, I, p. 25.
14. Luther, *Sermons,* I, p. 250.
15. *What Luther Says,* I, p. 347.
16. Benjamin Charles Milner, Jr., *Calvin's Doctrine of the Church,* Leiden: Brill, p. 100; Insti. IV.i.9.
17. Milner, *Calvin's Doctrine of the Church,* p. 121.
18. Milner, p. 119; *Insti.* IV.xiv.9. In contrast, consider Luther's statement: "They [the Zwinglians] divorced the Word and the Spirit, separated the person who preaches and teaches the Word from God, who works through the Word, and separated the servant who baptizes from God, who has commanded the Sacrament. They fancied that the Holy Spirit is given and works without the Word, that the Word merely gives assent to the Spirit, whom it already finds in the heart. If, then, this Word does not find the Spirit but a godless person, then it is not the Word of God. In this way they falsely judge and define the Word, not according to God, who speaks it, but according to the man who receives it. They want only that to be the Word of God which is fruitful and brings peace and life. . . ." *What Luther Says, II,* p. 664f. W-T 3, No. 868.
19. Milner, p. 128; *Insti.* IV.xvii.19.
20. Gregory L. Jackson, "Biblical Inerrancy: Summit III," *Christian News,* Dec. 22, 1986, p. 1.
21. *Christian Dogmatics,* II, p. 127; See also I, 25ff., III, 324.
22. Siegbert W. Becker, *The Foolishness of God, The Place of Reason in the Theology of Martin Luther,* Milwaukee: Northwestern Publishing House, 1982.

23. Pieper, *Christian Dogmatics*, I, p. 91.
24. *What Luther Says*, II, p. 572.
25. Luther, *Sermons*, III, p. 329; Pentecost, Third Sermon; John 14:23-31.
26. *What Luther Says* II, p. 915; W 17 II, 460; SL 11, 2325f.
27. Luther, *Sermons*, I, p. 99; Third Sunday in Advent; Mt. 11:2-10.
28. *What Luther Says*, I, p. 419; Eph. 6:10-17.
29. Luther, *Sermons*, IV, p. 282f.; Mt. 7:15-23.
30. Theodore E. Schmauk and C. Theodore Benze, *The Confessional Principle and the Confessions, as Embodying the Evangelical Confession of the Christian Church*, Philadelphia: General Council Publication Board, 1911, p. 685.
31. Otto Heick, *A History of Christian Thought*, 2 vols, Philadelphia: Fortress Press, 1966, II, p. 23.
32. Walther, *Law and Gospel*, p. 20-1.
33. Luther, *Sermons*, II, p. 305.
34. Luther, *Sermons*, II, p. 118.
35. Luther, *Sermons*, IV, p. 154; Fifth Sunday after Trinity; Lk 5:11.
36. Martin Luther, St. L. XIX, 1003f. Cited in *The Proper Distinction between Law and Gospel*, p. 306; Mt 7:18.
37. Heick, II, p. 24; emphasis added.
38. *The Proper Distinction between Law and Gospel*, pp. 362-363.
39. *Evangelische-Lutherische Dogmatik*, III, p. 253.
40. *What Luther Says*, III, p. 1270; W 40, I, 36f.; SL 9, 14; Preface, Galatians Commentary.
41. *What Luther Says*, III, p. 1269; W 30 II, 212; SL 14, 307f.
42. *Christian Dogmatics*, III, p. 161f.
43. *What Luther Says*, III, p. 1365; Gal. 5:9.
44. *What Luther Says*, I, p. 414.
45. *What Luther Says*, I, p. 412f.
46. *The Proper Distinction Between Law and Gospel*, p. 413.
47. *Sermons of Martin Luther*, 8 vols., III, p. 241.
48. *The Interpretation of St. Paul's First and Second Epistle to the Corinthians*, Columbus: Wartburg Press, 1946, p. 89.
49. *Sermons of Martin Luther*, II, p. 247 (Mk. 16:1-8).
50. Robert D. Preus, *The Theology of Post-Reformation Lutheranism*, two vols., St. Louis: Concordia Publishing House, 1970, I, p. 44.
51. *Concordia Triglotta*, St. Louis: Concordia Publishing House, 1921; Formula of Concord, SD, XI p.1095. Cited in Francis Pieper's, *The Difference between Orthodox and Heterodox Churches*, and Supplement, ed. Pastor E. L. Mehlberg, Coos Bay, Oregon: 1981, p. 65.

APPENDIX

The following books and periodicals are listed to help the reader pursue additional study in the area of doctrinal apostasy. They are listed in subject categories.

Apostasy

Barnhardt, David, *The Church's Desperate Need for Revival*, Eagan, Minnesota: Abiding Word Ministries, 1987. Barnhardt left the Lutheran Church in America and joined the Association of Free Lutheran Churches over the use of pornographic films by Lutheran Social Services of Minnesota.

Beck, Roy Howard, *On Thin Ice: A Religion Reporter's Memoir,* Wilmore: Bristol Books, 1988. Beck went to New York as a sympathetic reporter covering the National Council of Churches and had his eyes opened by homosexual activism and support for Marxism.

Hunsinger, George, ed., *Karl Barth and Radical Politics,* Philadelphia: Westminster Press, 1976. The essays show Barth's close ties with Marxism, starting with his first parish in Safenwill, Switzerland.

Hutcheson, Richard G., Jr., *Mainline Churches and the Evangelicals, A Challenging Crisis?* Atlanta: John Knox Press, 1981. The author, a liberal church executive, explored the reasons for mainline decline.

Jackson, Gregory L., "Out of the Depths of ELCA, A Pastor Looks at Lutheran Apostasy," *Christian News,*

February 9, 1987. The author left the Lutheran Church in America over the issues of inerrancy, abortion, and homosexual activism, and joined the Wisconsin Synod.

Jones, E. Michael, *Is Notre Dame Still Catholic? How Catholic Higher Education Has Failed the Church and Impoverished the Souls of Today's Students*, South Bend, Indiana: Fidelity Press, 1989. The editor of Fidelity, a conservative Roman Catholic magazine, shows how Notre Dame has become a mainline institution which openly denies the historic faith.

Kelley, Dean, *Why Conservative Churches Are Growing*, New York: Harper and Row, 1977. A National Council of Churches executive, Kelley charted the decline in membership which accompanied mainline church political activism.

LIFT, *What's Going Wrong Among the Lutherans*, (to be published). Lutherans Informed for the Truth, an independent group, formed to illustrate the differences between traditional, scriptural Lutheranism and the new thinking which opposes the inerrancy of the Bible.

Lindsell, Harold, *The Battle for the Bible*, Grand Rapids: Zondervan, 1976. Lindsell shocked the Evangelical world when he showed that many of their icons, including Fuller Seminary, had already abandoned the inerrancy of Scripture.

Marquart, Kurt, *Anatomy of an Explosion*, Grand Rapids: Baker Book House, 1977. Marquart explored the causes of the split in the Missouri Synod dramatized by the Seminex walkout in 1974.

Montgomery, John Warwick, ed., *Crisis in Lutheran Theology, the Validity and Relevance of Historic Lutheranism vs. Its Contemporary Rivals*, 2 vols.,

Minneapolis: Bethany Fellowship, 1967. These books alerted many people, including the author, to the doctrinal issues in Lutheranism.

Otten, Herman J., *Baal or God.* The editor of *Christian News* detailed the early growth of mainline rejection of the Bible as God's word.

_____, *Christian News Encyclopedia,* 4 vols., Washington, Missouri: the Missourian, 1982. These volumes are an unparalleled source of information about American Christianity.

Robb, W. Edmund, Julia Robb, *The Betrayal of the Church: Apostasy and Renewal in the Mainline Denominations,* Westchester: Crossways Books, 1986. The Robbs have shown the effects of political activism in the National Council of Churches and the World Council of Churches.

Schaeffer, Francis A., *The Great Evangelical Disaster,* Westchester, Illinois: Crossways Books, 1984. Schaeffer, an early pro-life activist, expressed his dismay over Evangelical commitment to doctrine.

Stanford, Craig, S., *The Death of the Lutheran Reformation, A Practical Look at Modern Theology and Its Effects in the Church and in the Lives of Its People,* Ft. Wayne: Stanford Publishing, 1988. Stanford left the ELCA after working with the Fellowship of Evangelical Lutheran Laity and Pastors (FELLP) and described his experiences with liberals and charismatics.

Stringfellow, William, and Anthony Towne, *The Death and Life of Bishop Pike,* Garden City: Doubleday and Company, 1976. Pike, an Episcopalian bishop, anticipated the openness of mainline professors and bishops today by attacking the Trinity, the virgin birth,

Appendix

and other central doctrines of the Bible. His unhappy personal life is chronicled in exquisite detail by close friend and lawyer William Stringfellow.

Webber, David Jay, "Will the New Lutheran Church Be Truly 'Lutheran?,' " *The Lutheran Synod Quarterly*, December, 1987, pp. 44-68. Reproduced in a booklet by the Evangelical Lutheran Synod, this essay compares ELCA doctrine to confessional Lutheranism.

The Bible

Arndt, William, *Bible Difficulties and Seeming Contradictions,* ed. Robert G. Hoerber and Walter Roehrs, St. Louis: Concordia Publishing House, 1987. Arndt used the difficult passages of the Bible to defeat the accusations of those who say the word of God is full of errors and contradictions.

Bultmann, Rudolph, and Five Critics, *Kerygma and Myth*, New York: Harper and Row, 1961. This volume proposed the century-old concept that the narratives of the Bible are myths, true in the universal sense but not necessarily historical.

Ehlke, Roland Cap, ed., *The People's Bible*, Milwaukee: Northwestern Publishing House. This multivolume popular commentary on the entire Bible is being written by Wisconsin Synod pastors and professors and aimed at the interested layman.

Lenski, R. C. H., *New Testament Commentary,* Minneapolis: Augsburg Publishing House, 1961. Lenski was a member of the old Ohio Synod, which is now a part of the Evangelical Lutheran Church in America. He taught at Capitol Seminary, now Trinity Lutheran Seminary. His commentaries display a remarkable knowledge of Greek and orthodox Lutheran doctrine. He taught the inerrancy of Scripture and made fun of the pseudo-scholarship of those who did not.

Luther, Martin, *Commentary on Galatians*, Grand Rapids: Kregel Publications, 1979. Luther's unexcelled clarity allows the reader to study Galatians to learn the dangers of legalism and the fruits of the Christian faith.

_____, *Commentary on Romans*, Grand Rapids: Kregel Publications, 1954. The person intimidated by heavy tomes on Romans can start with Luther's commentary and gain great insights with each page.

McDowell, Josh, *Evidence That Demands a Verdict, Historical Evidences for the Christian Faith*, 2 vols., San Bernardino: Here's Life Publishers, 1979. This is a convenient source of information about the reliability and historical accuracy of the Bible, though it tends to follow the Reformed concept of making the Scriptures reasonable.

Meier, Gerhard, *The End of the Historical-Critical Method*, trans. Edwin W. Leverenz and Rudolph F. Norden, St. Louis: Concordia Publishing House, 1977. Meier answers the claims of liberals who arbitrarily select which parts of the Bible are the Word of God.

Pieper, August, *Isaiah II, An Exposition of Isaiah 40-66*, trans. Erwin E. Kowalke, Milwaukee: Northwestern Publishing House, 1979. In this masterful commentary, Pieper addresses the liberal claims that two or three Isaiahs were combined.

Saarnivaara, Uuras, *Can the Bible Be Trusted? Old and New Testament Introduction and Interpretation*, Minneapolis: Osterhus Publishing House, 1983. This one-volume guide to the books of the Bible presents the traditional view of inerrancy and answers modern critics.

Church History

Aaberg, Theodore, *A City Set on a Hill, A History of the Evangelical Lutheran Synod,* Mankato, Minnesota: ELS Board of Publication, 1968. The history of the Evangelical Lutheran Synod, which emerged in protest against doctrinal compromise, illustrates how a church grows through the means of grace taught in purity and truth. The break-up of the old Synodical Conference is also described.

Ahlstrom, Sydney, *A Religious History of the American People*, New Haven: Yale University Press, 1972. This history of American religion, from a liberal perspective, has become a standard text.

Fendt, Edward C., *The Struggle for Lutheran Unity and Consolidation in the U.S.A. from the Late 1930s to the Early 1970s*, Minneapolis: Augsburg Publishing House, 1980. Fendt followed Lenski at Capitol Seminary, but worked toward merger based on compromise. His anecdotes offer many insights into Missouri's softening stance toward doctrine, led by William Arndt.

Forster, Walter O., *Zion on the Mississippi, The Settlement of the Saxon Lutherans in Missouri, 1839-1841,* St. Louis: Concordia Publishing House, 1953. This history of the Missouri Synod begins with the Bishop Stephan scandal and C. F. W. Walther's early leadership of the fledgling church body during a time of doctrinal crisis.

Fuerbringer, Ludwig, *Eighty Eventful Years, Reminiscences of Ludwig Ernest Fuerbringer*, St. Louis: Concordia Publishing House, 1944. Fuerbringer's historical sketches and memories of Walther and other early leaders make more poignant his son's role in turning over Concordia Seminary in St. Louis to John Tietjen and the liberals.

_____, *Persons and Events*, St. Louis: Concordia Publishing House. Fuerbringer's memories of Hoenecke and other Lutheran leaders remind us of the early struggles to establish genuine Lutheranism.

Koehler, John Philipp, *The History of the Wisconsin Synod*, ed. Leigh D. Jordahl, Sauk Rapids, Minnesota: Protes'tant Conference, 1981. Koehler describes in great detail the emergence of the Wisconsin Synod from the influences of Pietism and Unionism.

Nelson, E. Clifford, ed., *The Lutherans in North America*, Fortress: Philadelphia, 1975. This Lutheran history, though favoring the liberals, sorts out the mergers and compromises of the past, with many useful charts and quotations.

Wentz, Abdel Ross, *A Basic History of Lutheranism in America*, Philadelphia: Muhlenberg Press, 1955. Wentz favorably describes the trend toward confessional Lutheranism, which led to the formation of the United Lutheran Church in America in 1917, now part of the ELCA.

Cults
Ball, John, *Saints of Another God*, Milwaukee: Northwestern Publishing House, 1989. This is a good summmary of the strange doctrines of Mormonism.

Becker, Siegbert W., *Wizards That Peep, A Journey into the Occult,* Milwaukee: Northwestern Publishing House. Becker saw the dangers of the occult long before others took notice.

Harris, Jack, *Freemasonry, The Invisible Cult in Our Midst*, Towson, Maryland: Jack Harris, 1983. A former Masonic leader wrote about his discovery that the Masonic Lodge is anti-Christian, in spite of claims to the contrary.

Martin, Walter, *The Kingdom of the Cults*, Minneapolis: Bethany House Publishers, 1965. The most respected author on the subject of cults deals with many flourishing religions: Jehovah's Witnesses, Mormonism, Bahai, Worldwide Church of God, and Scientology.

_____, *The Maze of Mormonism*, Ventura, California: Regal, 1962. Martin's careful examination of Mormonism presents a devastating answer to claims that the Latter-day Saints are Christian.

_____, *The New Cults*, Ventura: Regal Books, 1980. Some of the cults uncovered by Martin include Silva Mind Control, EST, The Way International, and Transcendental Meditation.

Rice, John R., *Lodges Examined by the Bible, Is It a Sin to Have Membership in Secret Orders?* Murfreesboro, Tennessee, 1971. This is an older classic about the Masonic Lodge.

Schnell, William J., *Jehovah's Witnesses Errors Exposed*, Grand Rapids: Baker Book House, 1959. Schnell explains the strange doctrines of the Jehovah's Witnesses.

Spencer, James R., *Beyond Mormonism, An Elder's Story*, Old Tappan, New Jersey: Fleming Revell, 1984. Spencer found himself shunned and rejected when he began to question Mormonism and became a Christian, a dramatic and personal story.

Doctrine

Braaten, Carl, and Robert Jenson, ed., *Christian Dogmatics*, 2 vols., Philadelphia: Fortress Press, 1986. Six ELCA seminary professors reworked earlier publications into this starkly honest rejection of historic Christian teaching.

Chemnitz, Martin, *Examination of the Council of Trent*, 4 vols., trans. Fred Kramer, St. Louis: Concordia Publishing House, 1971. Chemnitz, a key leader in the Book of Concord effort, addresses the doctrinal errors of the Roman Catholic Council of Trent, which institutionalized Medieval errors.

_____, *On the Lord's Supper*, trans. Jacob A. O. Preus, St. Louis: Concordia Publishing House, 1979. This is Chemnitz' defense of the Real Presence, in opposition to Reformed errors.

_____, *The Two Natures of Christ*, trans. Jacob A. O. Preus, St. Louis: Concordia Publishing House, 1971. Chemnitz uses the Scriptures and the church fathers to present a clear picture of Christ's human and divine natures.

Concordance to the Book of Concord, ed. K. E. Larson, Milwaukee: Northwestern Publishing House, 1990. Every essential word is located in the Book of Concord, so that the layman or pastor can study issues in the confessions.

Concordia Triglotta, St. Louis: Concordia Publishing House, 1921.

Clouse, Robert, *The Church in the Age of Orthodoxy and Enlightenment, Consolidation and Challenge, 1600-1700*, St. Louis: Concordia Publishing House, 1980. This volume covers the seldom-studied era which followed Luther's work and the Book of Concord of 1580.

Heick, Otto, *History of Christian Thought*, 2 vols., Philadelphia: Fortress Press, 1966. Heick outlines doctrinal development from the church fathers to the modern era.

Hoenecke, Adolph, *Evangelische-Lutherische Dogmatik*, 4 vols., Milwaukee: Northwestern Publishing House, 1909. Soon to be published in English, Hoenecke is considered superior to Pieper's *Christian Dogmatics* in several respects.

Pieper, Francis, *Christian Dogmatics*, 3 vols., St. Louis: Concordia Publishing House. Pieper not only presents Lutheran doctrine but also shows where error has controverted the teaching of the Bible.

Preus, Robert, *The Theology of Post-Reformation Lutheranism,* 2 vols, St. Louis: Concordia Publishing House, 1972. No other book in print teaches so much about the men and the sound doctrine which rebuilt Lutheranism.

Schaller, John, *Biblical Christology*, Milwaukee: Northwestern Publishing House, 1919. This small volume clarifies the Bible's teaching about Christ and points out common errors.

Senkbeil, Harold L., *Sanctification: Christ in Action, Evangelical Challenge and Lutheran Response,* Milwaukee: Northwestern Publishing House, 1989. Senkbeil explores the temptations of getting rid of the means of grace in order to fit in with the pietism of the Evangelicals.

Walther, C. F. W., *The Proper Distinction Between Law and Gospel*, ed. W. H. T. Dau, St. Louis: Concordia

Publishing House. Walther's Luther lectures are the greatest contribution to theology in America, a guide to understanding evangelism, sermons, pastoral counseling, and the importance of rejecting false doctrine.

Wolf, Richard C., *Documents of Lutheran Unity in America*, Philadelphia: Fortress Press, 1966. These confessional statements allow the student to track the progress and retreat of confessional Lutheranism.

Evolution

Collin, Remy, *Evolution, Twentieth Century Encyclopedia of Catholicism*, vol. 30, New York: Hawthorn Books, 1959. Collin explains how the Roman Catholic Church has accommodated herself to the theory of evolution.

Denton, Michael, *Evolution: A Theory in Crisis,* Bethesda: Adler and Adler, 1985. Denton's work addresses the scientific problems with the theory of evolution.

Graebner, Theo, *Essays on Evolution*, St. Louis: Concordia Publishing House, 1925. Graebner, a Lutheran, opposed evolution in this volume.

Hofstadter, Richard, *Social Darwinism in American Thought*, Boston: Beacon Press, 1955. Hofstadter traces the development of evolutionary thought in America and the impact of Darwin.

McLoughlin, John C., *Archosauria, A New Look at the Old Dinosaur*, New York: Viking Press, 1979. This popular treatment shows how advanced and specialized the dinosaurs were, contrary to early evolutionary assumptions.

Morris, Henry M., *The Twilight of Evolution,* Grand Rapids: Baker Book House, 1963. Morris is a well-known representative of "scientific creationism," which owes much to Reformed doctrine.

Luther

Bainton, Roland, *Here I Stand, A Life of Martin Luther,* New York: Mentor Books, 1950. Bainton's association with the Quakers comes through in his misrepresentation of Luther on the Word. Many historical anecdotes about Luther and his times are worth reading.

_____, *Yale and the Ministry, A History of Education for the Christian Ministry at Yale from the Founding in 1701,* New York: Harper and Brothers, 1957. Bainton's honest history describes the victory of Unitarian doctrine in a school which was born conservative.

Becker, Siegbert W., *The Foolishness of God, The Place of Reason in the Theology of Martin Luther,* Milwaukee: Northwestern Publishing House, 1982. Becker shows how Luther placed reason in a ministerial or servant role below Scripture, instead of above or beside the Word.

Luther, Martin, *The Sermons of Martin Luther*, 8 vols., ed. John Lenker, Grand Rapids: Baker Book House, 1983. These sermons give an outstanding sample of Luther's emphasis on doctrine, his trust in the word, his humor, and the comfort derived from the gospel of Christ.

_____, *What Luther Says, An Anthology*, 3 vols, ed. Ewald Plass, St. Louis: Concordia Publishing House, 1959. Thousands of Luther's best quotations are combined with historical introductions and placed into subject categories.

Plass, Ewald, *This Is Luther*, St. Louis: Concordia Publishing House, 1984. This excellent study offers an accurate portrayal of the life of Luther.

Periodicals

Christian News, P. O. Box 241, Washington, MO 63090, an independent, conservative weekly. Editor: Pastor Herman Otten.

Concord, formerly *The Gay Lutheran*, official periodical of Lutherans Concerned, P. O. Box 10461, Ft. Dearborn Station, Chicago, IL 60610-0461.

Concordia Historical Institute Quarterly, 801 De Mun Avenue, St. Louis, MO 63105, featuring Missouri Synod history.

Evangel, the newspaper of The American Association of Lutheran Churches, P. O. Box 17097, Minneapolis, MN 55417. These churches broke with The American Lutheran Church and tend to embrace Pentecostalism.

Evangelical Synod Quarterly (official Evangelical Lutheran Synod journal), 47 N. Division Street, Mankato, MN 56001. Editor: Professor Wilhelm Peterson.

Forum Letter / Forum Journal, (independent, less liberal perspectives about ELCA and Missouri) 338 E. 19th St, NY, NY 10003. Editors: Rev. Russell Saltzman and Rev. Paul Hinlicky.

LIFT (Lutherans Informed For the Truth), P. O. Box 6574, Saginaw, MI 48608. These newsletters offer a comparison of orthodox Lutheran doctrine and ELCA doctrine, with copious citations from LCA and ALC books and educational materials.

Lutheran Commentator (independent, witty critiques of ELCA), P. O. Box 1093, Minnetonka, MN 55435-0093. Editor: Russell E. Saltzman.

The Lutheran (official ELCA magazine), 8765 W. Higgins Rd, Chicago, IL 60631. Editor: Rev. Ed Trexler. *ELCA Partners* is the official publication for professional workers.

Lutheran Science Institute Journal, 19545 102 St., Bristol, WI 53104. This WELS/ELS group explores scientific issues.

The Lutheran Witness (official magazine of the Lutheran Church Missouri Synod), 3558 S. Jefferson Ave., St. Louis, MO 63118.

The Northwestern Lutheran (official Wisconsin Synod magazine), 2929 N. Mayfair Road, Milwaukee, WI 53222. Editor: Rev. James Schaefer.

Religion and Democracy, published by the Institute for Religion and Democracy, 729 15th St. NW, Suite 900, Washington D. C. 20005. The newsletters offer independent critiques of mainline political radicalism, especially through the National and World Councils of Churches. Ed Robb and Rev. Richard Neuhaus are IRD leaders.

WELS Historical Institute Journal, 2929 N. Mayfair Road, Milwaukee, WI 53222, featuring Wisconsin Synod history.

Wisconsin Lutheran Quarterly (official Wisconsin Synod journal), 11831 N. Seminary Drive, Mequon, WI 53092. Editor: Professor Wilbert Gawrisch.